Grace and Mortgage

*The language of faith
and the debt of the world*

PETER SELBY

DARTON·LONGMAN + TODD

First published in 1997 by
Darton, Longman and Todd Ltd
1 Spencer Court
140-142 Wandsworth High Street
London SW18 4JJ

Reprinted 1997 and 1998

ISBN 0–232–52170–0

A catalogue record for this book is
available from the British Library

Thanks are due to SCM Press Ltd for permission to quote
from 'The Past' taken from Dietrich Bonhoeffer, *Letters and
Papers from Prison*.

Photoset by Intype London Ltd
Printed and bound in Great Britain by
Redwood Books, Trowbridge, Wiltshire

Grace and Mortgage

By the same author:

BeLonging: Challenge to a Tribal Church (1991)
Rescue: Jesus and Salvation Today (1995)

For my father, Frank Selby,
who cared deeply about these things

Contents

Foreword

Foreword by the Most Revd Njongonkulu Winston Ndungane,
Archbishop of Cape Town

When I first read Bishop Peter Selby's book *Look for the Living*,
I realised that I was reading something written by a kindred
spirit. It was not long after reading the book that I had the
pleasure of meeting Peter Selby in Cape Town, where he presented a lecture on Bonhoeffer's christology. From that lecture
has come an important resource as the Church takes a serious
look at the question of a world in debt. International debt is
something that is stifling human freedom and that has disastrous
consequences for our global family. The debilitating reality of
nations trapped in the consequences of debt creates, in my
opinion, another form of slavery. Again, it seems, the poor are
providing for the rich. Indeed the awesome burden of international debt causes, at the most extreme level, a loss of dignity
and hope.

This book is of the utmost importance. It is timely as we look
ahead to the next millennium and pray God that the call for
jubilee in that year will be recognised by the powers that be.
This will be a challenge as we respond to the call of Pope John
Paul II and indeed within the Anglican Communion during the
Lambeth Conference in 1998. It is incredible that with all the
issues facing our world today, international debt has come out
as the primary subject for discussion at the decennial Anglican
Meeting in Canterbury in 1998. Debt affects everyone. As I chair
the section of the Lambeth Conference entitled 'Called to Full
Humanity', I bring with me the prayers and concerns of a world
community. The worry of debt hampers economic strengthening
and thwarts human development. The elimination of debt is the
only way forward. In Southern Africa steps are being taken on
an ecumenical basis to move forward in addressing the issue of
poverty. This issue is too big for one individual or one Church
to take on, and at my enthronement celebration I begged my

fellow Church leaders to come together to be a united witness, to learn from and to respond to those who are enslaved by debt.

I believe it will take two or three generations to change. We must begin now. The Church could have a primary responsibility in undertaking education in this area and I believe it is indeed a call enabling us to make Christ known as Liberator and Saviour. Africans are deeply religious people and have a high doctrine of humanity. I pray that as we all look forward to the year 2000 we will claim that year for Jesus Christ with great enthusiasm, and remember the people of this world who are begging for a compassionate response from the world community because they look to a brighter future. We must remember that in many cases it was in a very unjust way that the debts were incurred in the first place: this issue is one of justice as well as simple wisdom if we wish the future to be a time in which we can use our freedom to respond to God in love.

I believe Peter Selby has given us the means whereby we can appropriately, through biblical reflection and proper education, move ahead to formulate a new way. Peter Selby is engaging us and encouraging us to be responsible stewards of God's creation. I believe that the timing of this book is perfect. I close with a few words from my enthronement sermon which I hope will lead you more fully into the pages ahead: '*It was a wounded Christ whom God made the instrument of healing in the world; by his wounds we have been healed (1 Peter 2:24). God has the power to transform agents of brokenness into agents of healing. He calls us to be agents of change in a broken world. He calls us to be angels of healing in a wounded society. As long as we have the poor, the hungry and the homeless in our society, there will never be any stability, we will never be at peace with ourselves.*'

† NJ Ungqukushe (ape Tum

Acknowledgements

This book is much occupied with debts and their severe consequences. Recognising indebtedness can also be a good thing to do, and without such an acknowledgement at its very beginning this book would be missing something vital. These debts cannot of course be repaid – they are not debts of that kind. But many people in a diversity of ways have been part of this project, and without them either it could not have happened or it would have been greatly impoverished.

For the period 1992–97 I have been privileged to hold the William Leech Professorial Fellowship in Applied Christian Theology at the University of Durham. The Fellowship was created as the result of the generosity and vision of Sir William Leech, of the Foundation that he established, and of the five charities that are its principal beneficiaries. That generosity and vision have not only made possible the reflection and research which have led to the writing of this book but have been a real inspiration in carrying it out.

The Fellowship also brought with it the continued support and encouragement of the Directors of the Foundation. What has particularly assisted the progress of my thinking has been the regular conversations I have had with the Fellowship Support Group: the members of that group – Professor Richard Bailey, Professor James Dunn, Dr Ruth Etchells, Bishop Kenneth Gill, the Revd Robin Hutt, the Revd John Mitchell, the Revd Dr John Polkinghorne and Professor Colin Russell – have offered me both individually and together an invaluable balance of affirmation and criticism as the task proceeded. The members of the group would acknowledge, as I gladly do, the very special contribution of time, energy and commitment by Nigel Sherlock, who has chaired the group throughout the period of my tenure, stewarding its resources, enabling its meetings, and always displaying the greatest interest in the work, at one point convening a most valuable meeting of business associates to offer advice and reflection.

The Fellowship also brought with it the rich intellectual friendship of my colleagues in the Theology Department of Durham University, all of whom have offered me the warmest of welcomes. I am particularly grateful to Dr Stephen Barton, Professor David Brown, Dr Colin Crowder, Dr Carol Harrison, Professor Ann Loades, Dr Walter Moberly, Dr Loren Stuckenbruck and Dr Alan Suggate for conversations, in some cases frequent ones, in which they have listened to my confusions and obsessions and pointed me in creative new directions. I have been enabled at times to try out some of these ideas in the Department's postgraduate seminars, to the members of which I am most grateful, especially to Christopher Devanny and Paul Fletcher, whose continued interest in my work and whose sharing of their own research have been invaluable.

Many others have volunteered their help. Dr John Selby, my brother, was always on the lookout for research material on debt, and Jeremy Carrette gave me vital leads from his own research and reflection. I have been touched by the willingness of others who scarcely knew me to interest themselves in this project: Alan Laurie has given me through correspondence and conversation an enormous amount of his deep reflection; Professor Stephen Lea of Exeter University shared with me his work on student and consumer debt. In the field of domestic debt, Avran Taylor introduced me to the research he was doing at Durham University into credit unions; I learned an enormous amount from Michael Wolfe about his own work at the Citizens' Advice Bureau, and, through material he obtained for me, of the huge burden of work in the field of debt carried by the Citizens' Advice Bureaux nationally. To have met Councillor Margaret Nolan and learned from her about the dimensions of her commitment to her community in North Tyneside and her tireless efforts in the establishment of credit unions was a great privilege. The Revd Dr Graham Blount has been researching into domestic debt for many years, and his willingness to share his personal knowledge, to encourage my exploration and to let me have his PhD thesis were of immense assistance.

Those who have studied and campaigned about the issues presented by the international debt crisis have also allowed my enquiries to interrupt them and have been generous with their time and insight. I am particularly grateful to Martin Dent of JUBILEE 2000, Ann Pettifor of the Debt Crisis Network, and

Tim Moulds and Paul Spray of Christian Aid. As I write this, there are signs that the scourge of international debt (which I have tried here to suggest is closely related to the similar scourge of domestic debt) might receive some appropriate attention and mitigation; I hope and pray so, and that the insights which they have been willing to share with me as this work has proceeded may be grasped widely and may lead to effective remedies.

I am grateful to publishers who have permitted me to include here versions of material that has appeared in other guises on other occasions: Chapter 2 is a revision partly of material first presented here in Durham in a lecture to celebrate the fiftieth anniversary of Dietrich Bonhoeffer's death, and partly of a lecture, 'Who is Jesus Christ for us today?', given at the Seventh International Bonhoeffer Congress in Cape Town in January 1996, which now appears in *Bonhoeffer for a New Day: theology in a time of transition* (Grand Rapids, Eerdmans, 1997). Chapter 4 is an adaptation of 'Love in the city', one in a volume of essays, *Essentials of Christian Community* (Edinburgh, T. & T. Clark, 1996), edited by David F. Ford and Dennis L. Stamps, in honour of Daniel Hardy, to whose constant encouragement I owe a great deal; and Chapter 6 contains a section from 'What Simeon said . . . and Anna was waiting for', from 'The Gospel, the Poor and the Churches', a number of the *Christian Action Journal* published in 1995 to celebrate the golden jubilee of Christian Aid, as well as an extract from an article written for the *Church Times* in July 1996. John Nicholson, a long-standing friend and conversation-partner about many things including this research, has kindly agreed to my sharing a snatch of his privately published *Words to a Liberating God*, a much treasured gift, with a wider public.

Professor Duncan Forrester and the Revd Andrew Morton of the Centre for Theology and Public Issues at Edinburgh have been generous in their interest, and Professors Richard Bauckham and Trevor Hart and Dr Timothy Gorringe, of the University of St Andrews, offered me a valuable opportunity to try out my ideas. Conferences with the Dioceses of Carlisle and Southwell came at a crucial point, and I greatly appreciated their responsiveness, as well as the opportunity which those invitations gave me of collaborating with Dr Marcella Althaus-Reid and the Revd Alison White.

I was particularly delighted to have the opportunity to discuss my reflections on the place of money with Dr John Baker, formerly Bishop of Salisbury, to whose care in my earliest exploration of Christian faith I owe so much, and to receive from him his translation of the relevant passage of Theodor Bovet's writing on the subject. It was also a pleasure and privilege throughout this project to be meeting with Dr David Jenkins, formerly Bishop of Durham and now Honorary Professor in the Department of Theology there, and sharing his valuable insight into the connections between faith and economy.

I gladly acknowledge how fortunate I was in having two particular 'theological friends' – an expression intended to convey that they are much more than theologians who happen to be friends, or friends who happen to be theologians. Professor Christopher Rowland, of Oxford University, knows better than most the sense of risk that constantly invaded me in the attempt to hold together the strands which are each essential to my developing argument. Dr Alistair McFadyen, of Leeds University, undertook to be my adviser and consultant throughout my tenure of the Fellowship; his constant, supportive interest and critical judgement made our sessions together a crucial catalyst of what has emerged. And for their perceptive companionship in the inner struggles that accompanied this project, I can only say 'thank you' to Ralph Blundell and Canon Kate Tristram, and it is deeply felt.

The decision to do this research involved those closest to me in all that goes with moving to the other end of the country, and then living with the mood-swings and midnight oil which, for me at any rate, are involved in writing a book. I am deeply grateful to Jan, my wife, for being willing to make the many train journeys which that move cost her at the time when it happened, and for her incredible patience. Ben, Susi and Naomi were all affected in different ways by my pursuit of this project; the way they bore that means a huge amount.

My father, Frank Selby, was always deeply interested in my work, and on the area of economics and the values at stake read widely and formed his own passionate judgements. I am sad that he died before the book was finished, and treasure his annotations on parts of it that I had shown him. It would have been good to know whether (as I hope) he would have agreed with much that I have written, and to have had some good arguments about the rest. This book is an offering in his memory, a sign perhaps of the possibility that the world could be a place where debts, especially those that are too large to describe let alone think of repaying, can yet be occasions of delight and thankfulness.

Durham. Advent 1996   Peter Selby

I

What this book is and how it happened

It was a disturbing programme that accompanied the cooking of supper. The investigation of how horticultural workers in Kenya were having their health ruined by the pesticides they were compelled to use to produce everything from roses to pineapples for European tables was disturbing enough. The questions it raised about the price being paid by those workers to enable the consumers in wealthier lands to have what they want at any time of the year when they want were sharp and serious. So were the evasive responses of international food companies about the safety and health of their workers.

Yet more disturbing still were the efforts which the Kenyan government felt it had to make to discourage (to put it mildly) the investigative team from discovering what was happening and reporting it. Why would this be? Would it not be in their interests to have the damage being done to their people's health exposed? Sadly not, it seemed. What was clear was that more basic than the provision of pineapples out of season for the world's wealthier consumers was the servicing of loans from public and private sources which supported the economies of poorer countries. If questions were raised about the safety of horticultural workers, eventually Kenya's ability to service, let alone repay, its debts would be damaged, and new loans would not be forthcoming. From the point of view of the internal politics of the country, that would be bound eventually to lead to social and political unrest. Hence the government's concern to keep things quiet.

In fact, however, by the time I heard that programme I had already found myself drawn into more and more concern about indebtedness and its ramifications. It would be good to be able to say that this concern had been aroused first in relation to the problems facing the world's poorest people. I had indeed known something of such matters; but what precipitated this increasing interest in the topic was an event that addressed me at a far more personal – and less altruistic – level: in November 1993, Kenneth

Clarke, the Chancellor of the Exchequer, included in his budget a reduction in student maintenance grants of ten per cent per annum for three years, with a commensurate increase in the student loans which those receiving higher education were to be encouraged to take. He deserves, though he would not appreciate it, a place on my acknowledgements page; for his action provoked in me, initially as a parent of a student, some uncomfortable reflections.

What, after all, would be the by-product of a system that ensured that all students would collect in the course of their studies not just an education and a degree, but also a steadily increasing debt? Surely an inevitable effect – a cynic might dare to suggest also the obvious intention – would be the engendering of a climate of conformity and compliance in those who knew that whatever else they wished to do with their lives, eventually they would certainly have to repay their debt. Is it possible for those encumbered with debt to maintain a critical, even rebellious, attitude to the society in which they live? Whether intentionally or not, an indebted student body would be very strongly discouraged from initiating anything like the disturbances which rocked the world of higher education in 1968.

My train of thought lumbered on. After all, it was not only students who faced a constantly growing mountain of debt. An equally obvious, and much larger, group of 'debtors' (though, as we shall see, people with debts do not always see themselves as debtors; whether they see themselves in that light depends on a variety of factors) were those who had been tempted to join the 'property-owning democracy' which had been around a long time, but which was a particular feature of the political programme of the 1980s. They – I, as a fellow mortgagor, should say 'we' – were likewise tied by their debt into an accepting and compliant attitude to the world around them. What could be more stifling to a sense of vocation, to the forces of social criticism, or even to enterprise, than the knowledge of being beholden to your creditors? (There is a paradox here: for the same period that saw a vast increase in the amount of mortgage debt was also a time when we were exhorted to join the 'enterprise culture'.) It is not hard to imagine a contemporary scenario in which Jesus, inviting someone to become a follower of his, receives a reply not about a father to bury or a yoke of oxen to prove but about a mortgage to pay off.

Pursuing these reflections about the effect of indebtedness turned out to be highly revealing: debt brings about a power relationship and creates a 'bond' (the word is significant) that is often unequal and constraining. That is true whether we are speaking about a personal debt, about communities in our own society with a 'debt problem', or about the much remarked 'international debt crisis'.

Usually it is the debtor who is in the weak position, but not always. If your debt is large enough and the threat of your reneging on that debt therefore serious enough, then you can, as a debtor, be in a position of power. So, for example, the debts owed by Eurotunnel on the construction of the Channel Tunnel became so large at one point that their bankers could not afford to refuse to reschedule their payments. Similarly the proposals to renegotiate the debts of poorer countries came about because the scale of their debts and the likelihood of non-payment became so great that very serious consequences were staring banks in the wealthier countries in the face. Likewise it became clear in the late 1980s and early 1990s that the collapse in house prices was such that if nothing were done by the mortgage lenders the scale of arrears would become unbearable and that the repossession of properties where payments were in arrears would not protect the banks and building societies from loss.

Yet what appear from time to time as 'crises' are but a minute proportion of the massive role that debt and indebtedness play in our lives. Indeed the crises are really only so called because they are occasions when the normal relationship of power created by debt, in which the creditor has power over the debtor in a dynamic that is never questioned, is for some reason reversed. Most of the time debts are incurred, interest charges are levied and principal sums repaid without our considering that anything untoward has happened.

It has not always been so. As we shall see later, our forebears took a very much harsher view of the practice of lending money at interest. Not only was that so for a large part of Christian history, but such attitudes are a feature of Judaism and Islam as well. Furthermore, we do not have to delve into the ancient wisdom of the world's religions to find a time when the attitude to debt in our own culture was radically different. The encouragement of thrift, the discouragement of debt, and the view that loans should be repaid as soon as possible have been a feature of life for most of our own century, not simply an example of 'Victorian values'. When dominant politicians in the 1980s propounded the notion that public debt was a bad thing, and took measures to reduce public borrowing and even to repay parts of the national debt, they were able to appeal to this well-rooted instinct – while passing quickly over the fact that private debt was increasing at a massive rate during the same period.

To these matters we shall need to return in later chapters. First, however, more must be said about how these observations about debt affected the theological explorations I was undertaking at the time when they first struck me. For despite its importance as an issue for people of faith, the subject of this book is not debt in and of itself, but debt as a key term for understanding the person of Christ in our time. For some time I had been reflecting on the famous question put by Dietrich Bonhoeffer in the letter he wrote from prison on 30 April 1944, who Christ really is for us today.[1] It is one of those questions which can leap off the page on which it was written and form the basis of prolonged reflection irrespective of its original context or what its author might have meant.

So it might have been; but as it turned out, and as will appear later, Bonhoeffer's own context and the background of his thinking form a crucial framework for dealing with his question. He proposes in his letters some demanding criteria for what would count as an adequate answer to his own question. Two in particular are inescapable: Christian faith has to address a world in which its everyday activity is undertaken on largely secular assumptions; and the gospel has to address human beings in their strength rather than creating and then exploiting a sense of weakness.

These two criteria have a great deal to do with the way in which the language of debt has come to be used in Christian doctrine and piety. For the theme of humanity as in debt to God, and of Jesus as having in some sense been the repayment of that debt, is an extremely prominent one. It might be said to have become one of the most frequent metaphors used to convey the meaning of the death of Christ, so much so that it has come to be regarded as scarcely a metaphor at all, but simply a statement of the human condition.

The same process which has led to its being scarcely seen as a metaphor at all has also led to the loss of any real connection with what being in debt is actually like. Do people using the petition in the Lord's Prayer, 'Forgive us ... as we forgive ...', connect it with the experience of telling the water company that they cannot pay their bill, or the building society that they cannot afford the repayments? Do we see in those words any connection with the escalating level of credit card debt, or the simultaneous proclaiming of the economic theory that public debt leads to inflation and must be reduced at all costs, while private debt can safely be left to find its own level in the market?

As we shall see, the language of debt has come to be a powerful metaphor in many areas of life, and one which, again, hardly seems metaphorical at all. The language of morality is full of notions of indebtedness. In languages with a Latin root, the same root *debita* stands for debt and for duty; in the German, guilt and indebtedness are alike conveyed by *Schuld*. We often speak of duties as things we 'owe', and can describe ourselves as 'indebted' even when we have not borrowed anything and there is no expectation of repayment. In using such language we have often lost touch with the roots of the metaphor in actual financial transactions, and frequently cannot tell to what extent assumptions derived from the economic roots of the idea are continuing to operate even in situations which we should not like to think were economic at all.

In the wide-ranging nature of this metaphor has lain much of its religious power. The declaration that humanity is in debt has often preceded the 'good news' that Christ has paid off that debt. That presupposes of course that the sense of indebtedness will be recognised by the hearer; and it fails to take into account that the news that someone has, at the cost of his life, 'paid off' the debt you owed can simply enhance the sense of indebtedness you feel.

It is here that Dietrich Bonhoeffer's two criteria for a satisfactory answer to the question 'Who really is Jesus Christ for us today?' begin to demonstrate their importance. For his contention is that the discovery of what he called a 'new language, perhaps quite non-religious, but liberating and redeeming'[2] depends on using language that has recovered its lost connection with the dominant realities of everyday (secular) life. Secondly, it also depends on speaking in a way that addresses human beings in their strength.

So on the one hand the language of debt, if it is to be used, has to be based on a serious consideration of what debt is like in the real world people inhabit and of the transactions they carry out within it; and on the other hand the task of discovering language that speaks about Christ in ways that address human strength means focusing on humanity as *creditor* and not just as *debtor*. We are not simply those who have incurred debts we cannot repay; we are also those who drive hard bargains, who profit from the debts of others and who, perhaps most seriously of all, are implicated in and frequently dependent upon the flourishing of an economic system that has as its inevitable and disastrous consequence the reduction of many of our fellow men and women to a destitution from which there is no escape. Recent events in the money markets, including the collapse of major international banking institutions, led me also to look more closely at how the credit market actually works – and as we shall see, in that area of life all is very far from being what it seems.

My contention is that it is not an accident that we have lost touch with the roots of one of the most important metaphors that have been used about the person and work of Christ. For by seeing our debt to God and Christ's repayment of that debt as a spiritual truth (by which we easily mean, strangely for Christian believers, a truth that is not based in the material world) we are allowed to leave the financial world to look after itself and go its own way. We have made it possible for ourselves to worship God (religiously) and Mammon (economically) by simply allowing ourselves two separate kinds of language and not letting them interact in any way that would confront our dependence on the economy of credit.

Meanwhile the two kinds of language do continue to interact, but only in one direction: the religious speech about indebtedness continues to impress upon those who use it the overriding requirement that debts are to be repaid, while it says nothing to the world of credit about the still more overriding requirement to secure release for the world's most vulnerable from intolerable obligations. The language of faith is thereby used to offer reassurance to those who see themselves as indebted while requiring them to continue to pay their debts; meanwhile what we shall see as the enhancement of the power of the economy of credit proceeds unchecked.

For the gospel that the world, our place within it, our relationships with each other and our righteousness towards God are all *gift* represents a hard saying for us when we profit from (and the word 'profit' here has its full economic significance) an economy based on credit. This book is an attempt to expose some of the hardness of that saying because of the further ramifications the economy of credit has in our dealings with each other, that is in conditioning the shape of our relationships. As an explanation of the psychological and social origins of the sense of obligation and of guilt Friedrich Nietzsche's words may seem one-sided and simplistic, but there is a brutal frankness about them which bears witness to the power of the debt and credit relationship:

> The feeling of guilt . . . and of personal obligation has . . . its origin in the oldest and most primitive personal relationship which ever existed, the relationship between buyer and seller, creditor and debtor. Here for the first time person stood face to face with person, here for the first time person *weighed itself with person*.[3]

If such a statement fails as a simple historical explanation, it speaks very strongly as a myth that pervades human relationships when they go wrong: how many are those that are soured by the sense of something owed that cannot be repaid but that will always be mentioned or hinted at? How many are the hours that people have spent in therapy because of some person in their life, most likely a parent, whom they could never please enough or adequately recompense for all that they 'owed'? On the other hand, we also know of debts that do not have that overwhelming and constraining character: we often have a sense of being 'indebted' to someone whom we want to acknowledge (as with many books, this one begins with such 'acknowledgements') not because we feel bound and constrained by them, but simply because we want to recognise what we have received from others. At the heart of the aim of this book is the attempt to see what is the difference between debts that constrain and debts that delight, and how it is that the person and work of Christ might be seen as part of that difference.

Yet I shall suggest that the basic form and substance of indebtedness, that is to say the debts we owe in money, must never be far from our minds if we are to understand these wider ramifications. It is precisely our reluctance to speak about money that witnesses to its importance, our unwillingness often to borrow money from or lend money to people we regard as friends that witnesses to the power it has (we suspect) to tarnish fruitful encounters; we do not wish in the company of those whom we care most about to be in the position of 'person weighing itself with person'.

We shall also see that the processes of credit and debt have had a catastrophic effect on the way in which we relate to the natural world we share with animals, plants and other creatures. We are living, it seems, as those who think they hold a credit card with no limit to their credit and no date by which repayment will have to be made. We inhabit our universe increasingly as those who have a mortgage they can add to at will and will never have to discharge. This is a subtle, but in fact complete, reversal of what was meant by the traditional assertion that the world is in fact 'on loan'[4] to us or 'held in trust'.

The next chapters have therefore to range widely: we begin with an examination of some of Dietrich Bonhoeffer's most seminal thoughts about how the Christian gospel is to be witnessed to in a changed world context, and how the issue of debt and credit, about which he did not in fact speak, connects closely with one of his key ideas. We shall then look at the reality of the debt economy, its casualties on the world scale and more locally, probing the reality of indebtedness to see which are the myths and which the realities. We shall then need to examine the sources of much of what is said about the life and death of Christ in order to see whether approaching his life through the question of debt and credit is just an eccentric modern idea or whether, as I shall suggest, this corresponds remarkably closely to how he was heard in the first place and how the traditions about him and about the Church's teaching about money arose and developed.

Only then might it be possible to see whether Bonhoeffer's quest for a 'new language [about Christ and the gospel], perhaps quite non-religious' might emerge from what we have to say about debt and credit, and what the meaning of that discovery might be for our politics and economics, our praying and our discipleship. For the language of gift and debt (we may say of grace and mortgage), of mercy and demand, of forgiveness and judgement, of calling to account and remission of dues, all turns out to be deeply embedded not simply in the debates about 'social ethics' – what the gospel *im*plies, or how it can be *ap*plied – but in the way in which that gospel has been understood and the Christ at the centre of it has been understood. There is more of a connection between what we now call the 'economy' and what has traditionally been called the 'divine economy' than we have often supposed; and we shall only be following the example of Christ in many of the parables if we proceed on the basis that within the workings of trade, loan, accounting and the like lie powerful images of the kingdom of heaven.

Regain your whole image

Evil comes into my eye and soul;
what I see, I hate;
I hate what moves me;
all that lives I hate, all that is lovely,
all that would recompense me for my loss.
I want my life;
I claim my own life back again,
my past,
yourself.
Yourself. A tear wells up and fills my eye;
can I, in mists of tears,
regain your whole image,
yourself entire?[1]

The poem from which these lines come, *Vergangenheit*, 'The
Past', was written in late May of 1944 by Dietrich Bonhoeffer,
pastor, thirty-eight years old, prisoner in cell 92 at Tegel Prison.
It was smuggled out in draft to his friend, former pupil and later
editor and biographer, Eberhard Bethge, and then to the person
to whom it was addressed, his fiancée Maria von Wedemeyer. It
is the poem of a lover to a beloved after a prison visit, as its
opening lines make very clear:

O happiness beloved, and pain beloved in heaviness,
you went from me.
What shall I call you? Anguish, life, blessedness,
part of myself, my heart – the past?
The door was slammed;
I hear your steps depart and slowly die away.
What now remains for me – torment, delight, desire?
This only do I know: that with you, all has gone.

Love poem as it is, however, the four words taken from it as the
title of this chapter are a fitting summary of Bonhoeffer's stance
towards life and his quest to offer an account of the gospel that

speaks its truth in and to the modern world. In doing so they also headline at least one of the criteria which an engagement with Bonhoeffer establishes for finding a way of speaking of Jesus Christ in our time. A christology for our time must seek to speak to humanity in its strength, must not exploit human weakness, must, in short, support rather than undermine humanity's quest to regain its 'whole image'. For, as I indicated in the opening chapter, it was from Bonhoeffer's quest for a way of speaking of Jesus Christ in today's world – a contemporary christology – that I set out on the exploration that has led to the writing of this book. In this chapter I shall look in some depth at the demanding standard Bonhoeffer sets for confessing Jesus Christ today.

Let us begin with his original question:

> What is bothering me incessantly is the question what Christianity really is, or indeed who Christ really is, for us today. The time when people could be told everything by means of words, whether theological or pious, is over, and so is the time of inwardness and conscience – and that means the time of religion in general.[2]

Such is the struggle of a theologian confronted with modernity: what does the Christian inheritance amount to in the non-religious world we now inhabit? Paradoxically, it is of course a question most people would regard as 'religious'; you would not ask it if you were not yourself steeped in, and deeply preoccupied with, Christianity itself and its possibilities for today. Indeed it is precisely the situation of today that appears to vindicate Bonhoeffer's early perception, one in which he appears very much to speak with strong echoes of Karl Barth, that there is a profound contrast between on the one hand what the Christian revelation and the community which bears Christ's name stand for, and on the other the realm of religion and religious community. As he wrote in *Sanctorum Communio*:

> [Christianity] was not a new religion seeking adherents, which is a picture drawn by a later time. But God established the reality of the church, of mankind pardoned in Jesus Christ. Not religion, but revelation, not a religious community, but the church: that is what the reality of Jesus Christ means.[3]

In asking the question of Jesus Christ in this way, Bonhoeffer clearly has in mind the need to present the gospel credibly today, an agenda traditionally called apologetics. Yet on other occasions he asks the same question, how to speak of Jesus Christ, in a quite contrasting way, one which is equally christological but is presented, it seems, in a quite different tone of voice. This second agenda brings with it a different kind of passion, that of obedience and discipleship, and a language which we might call 'prophetic' rather than 'apologetic'. Here is that prophetic agenda as it was expressed in one of Bonhoeffer's very earliest public utterances, his statement to the congregation in Barcelona. Here are words of an assistant pastor aged merely twenty-two. This person is not wondering whether in this time Christ might have relevance, only how the life and demand of Christ can be expressed and responded to. This is not the Christ whose relevance to today's world is in any doubt; all that is in doubt is whether we shall make an adequate response:

> Whether in our time Christ can still occupy a place where we make decisions on the deepest matters known to us, over our own life and over the life of our people, that is the question we will consider today. Whether the Spirit of Christ has anything final, definitive, and decisive to say to us, that is what we want to speak about. We all know that Christ has in effect been eliminated from our lives. Of course we build him a temple, but we live in our own houses. Christ has become a matter of the church, or rather of the churchiness of a group, not a matter of life. Religion plays for the psyche of the nineteenth and twentieth centuries the role of the so-called Sunday room into which one gladly withdraws for a couple of hours but only to get back to one's work immediately afterwards. However, one thing is clear: we understand Christ only if we commit ourselves to him in a stark 'Either-Or'. He did not go to the cross to ornament and embellish our life. If we wish to have him, then he demands the right to say something decisive about our entire life.[4]

This form of the question 'Who really is Jesus Christ for us today?' resonates much more immediately with the needs of those faced with structures of oppression requiring resistance. The 'decisions about our lives and the lives of our people' are surely decisions about justice and truth in our relations with one another, about our participation in the ordering of our society and about our responsibility within the teeming variety of the living and material world. Here is a voice that echoes in the experience of the churches of the poor and their theologians of liberation who have followed on in the history of resistance since Bonhoeffer. This is not the perplexity of a post-Christian, post-Enlightenment, European Christianity, but a summons for the hour of radical discipleship more obviously and immediately relevant to the experience of Christians in the Two-Thirds World.

The contrast of these two agendas, old world perplexity and new world resistance, is perceived clearly in the way in which John de Gruchy explains the nature of Bonhoeffer's relevance for South Africa in the days of its struggle:

> We have not referred at all in this essay to Bonhoeffer's thinking in prison about Christianity in a 'world come of age'. The reason for this is that his earlier writings appear to be more relevant to our present situation. Moreover, there is a sense in which the Enlightenment as an historical event has passed us by at the southern tip of Africa, and therefore we are still a religious rather than a secular society.[5]

So the question with which de Gruchy's essay ends, 'Who is Jesus Christ for you in South Africa, today?'[6] surely has a quite different feel there from the one it conveys when it is asked by Bonhoeffer in general terms in the April 1944 letter. It certainly sounds very different from the way in which I heard it, in common with many of my contemporaries, when Dietrich Bonhoeffer first entered our consciousness.

For my own introduction to Bonhoeffer happened in the period which de Gruchy designates that of the 'creative misuse of Bonhoeffer'.[7] That is to say, I am conscious of belonging to the generation of those whose introduction to Bonhoeffer came through the flurry of debate occasioned by John Robinson's *Honest to God*. That was how it was that, as a student in 1963, I found myself grasping hold of the notions of 'a world come of age' and 'religionless Christianity' with enthusiasm. I had in those days little time for what I thought was the very conservative over-reaction of the practitioners of theology, a subject I had not then studied. Not only did the New Testament scholar

Dr George Caird declare in an Ascension Day sermon that St
Luke had pulled Dr Robinson's leg and it had come off in his
hand; but a few months later this douche of cold water
threatened, as I saw it, permanently to wash away my excitement:

> There is an immense amount of material in the Fathers,
> both Western and Eastern, which, taken along with the
> insights of the great mystical writers and masters of the spiri-
> tual life, should remind us first very sharply and then very
> profitably of the scandalous poverty of much modern
> 'theism'. The true extent of the scandal is peculiarly well
> shown by the fact that not only does the theism against
> which he [Bishop John Robinson] protests seem to very
> many people to be recognisably the theism of the Christian
> Church (and the only possible theism – hence the need for
> atheism) but he seems to be trapped in this belief himself.[8]

Those words were written by David Jenkins, whom I then
supposed to be some kind of a reactionary, such was the heat
generated in that debate which seems so long ago![9] Part of the
reason why the debate seems so distant in the current British
situation is the sense of religious optimism which pervaded much
of what liberal theologians were saying at that time. We now
know the truth of Michael Ramsey's comment to the Conference
of Modern Churchmen only four years after *Honest to God*,
when he drew attention to a secularism far more radical than
the liberal theological tradition was disposed to take into account.
That conference was entitled, significantly for our purposes,
Christ for Us Today. Ramsey pointed out how profound was the
scepticism which the secularism of that period was bringing to
such an agenda. In his opening sermon he said:

> It is not only how we understand the story of Jesus in
> relation to God and man, and how we find Jesus to be
> meaningful. Rather are men and women asking how man
> is meaningful at all, and whether the idea of meaningfulness
> has any validity in the world in which we live.[10]

Some thirty years later we know how hardened many of our
societies are to such questions, let alone to the answers which
Christianity has offered to them. We have also seen the
flourishing of fundamentalisms, Christian and other, which
suggest that for many the proper response of religion to mod-

ernity is strident confrontation. That implies a need to transcend the reading of Bonhoeffer which was the way in which many of us came to know him.

If our religious situation is different from that of 1943 or 1963, the politics with which many of us are confronted have altered too. Recent years have certainly witnessed some remarkable developments on the world scene, not least the transformations that have taken place in the governments of Central and Eastern Europe, and the bringing to an end of the apartheid regime in South Africa. Nonetheless it is hard not to balance any relief with some fear and trembling based on our own British experience, that the victories which have been so painfully achieved against totalitarian ideologies and regimes based on racial domination may be replaced by the sophisticated tools of modern capitalism. In his account of *Christianity and Democracy*, John de Gruchy must occasion a shiver of recognition when he writes about the ambiguous relationship between democracy and the free market ideology:

> Neo-conservatives such as Friedrich von Hayek and Milton Friedman, and other proponents of the new world order such as Francis Fukuyama, are adamant in their insistence on a market free from any kind of social control. For this reason, many advocates of the free market, such as Hayek, resist the checks and balances of democracy, even while using the freedoms it offers to achieve their own goals.[11]

It is not hard to read such an account as a description of what has happened in Britain in the last decade and a half.

More to the point, his words remind me of a meeting I attended at a hotel in downtown Bulawayo where a large gathering of business people – almost all white – was addressed by a spokesperson of a large South African corporation. His message was simple and clear: 'You people have done good business here; we need a settlement with the ANC and we'll have good business too, and yours will be even better.' My rejoicing at the power of economic pressure to change racist policies was, to say the least, tarnished somewhat by the equal foreboding at the capacity of those with economic power to exploit the possibilities – and avoid incurring the costs – of almost any political change.

We see therefore two somewhat different readings of Bonhoeffer, the prophet of humanity come of age, and the martyr of the resistance to racist tyranny, both in some measure vulnerable to the pressure of our new day. Like any large person whose life and thought is used to suit the various purposes of subsequent generations, Bonhoeffer is likely to survive these more or less 'creative misuses' and be read again; but for us the question presses hard: *are we* (as his present-day readers) *able to present a credible proclamation of the gospel in the modern world*?

The famous form of the christological question as it was posed in the April 1944 letter and which has been the governing question of my own theological explorations offers its own particular way of addressing the crucial matter of the continuing possibility of presenting Christ credibly in the modern world. It offers three words, 'who?', 'us' and 'today', to pose thereby three profound challenges to our continuing ability to speak credibly of Jesus Christ: the challenges of identity, of discernment and of solidarity. It is to these three challenges that I shall attend in the next three sections.

'Who?' – the challenge of identity

The question *Who*? runs like a thread through the whole history of Bonhoeffer's christological thinking. So in his reconstructed christology lectures he begins his 'positive christology' with the statement, 'The question may not run, "How is it possible to conceive of the Incarnate?", but "Who is he?" '[12] Similarly, later on in considering the humiliation and exaltation of Christ, he says, 'The question is no longer, "*How* can God be humiliated man?" but rather "*Who* is the humiliated God-man?" '[13]

In coming to this point, he has followed the lines he had sketched out for himself early in the lectures:

The question 'Who?' is the question of transcendence. The question 'How?' is the question of immanence. Because the one who is questioned here is the Son, the immanent question cannot grasp him. Not, 'How are you possible?' – that is the godless question, the serpent's question – but 'Who are you?' The question 'Who?' expresses the strangeness and otherness of the encounter and at the same time reveals itself as the question of the very existence of the enquirer himself.[14]

He elucidates the significance of this point in his reference to what a factory-worker might mean in asking about Jesus. Is Jesus (he would want to know) the one in solidarity with the worker in his opposition to the oppressions of capitalism, or is he the one so commonly represented by the Church as settled into bourgeois society?[15] Equally Bonhoeffer presents the issue of identity through the person of Dostoevsky's *Idiot*:

The idiot does not keep himself apart, but clumsily causes offence everywhere. He has nothing to do with the great ones, but with the children. He is mocked, and he is loved. He is the fool and he is the wise man. He endures all and he forgives all. He is revolutionary, yet he conforms. He does not want to – but he draws attention to himself simply by being there. Who are you? Idiot or Christ?[16]

We must note that the question of identity is in this connection mutual; those who examine the identity of the Christ will find their own identity questioned. Thus the encounters we see in the gospels go to the heart of the question of identity. Jesus' audience asks of him, 'Who is this?' only to find themselves facing basic questions about who *they* are; the answer to 'Are you the Christ?' is inevitably, 'Are you first of all a rich person, or a landowner, or a fisherman? Or are you first of all a human being?'

To engage seriously with the question of how a christology is possible for our time confronts us with just such personally demanding issues. We are drawn away from questionings about how the incarnation is to be explained, that is to say how the God-man, the first claim on our life and loyalty, is possible, and towards the issue of *Who is he*? The discipleship of prayer and action cuts through the doctrinal quest for how a Christ might be possible to the requirement to discern *who* Christ is – Christ or idiot? And having discerned, to face the question, *Who are you*?

The question asked in prison is not different from this: in a world that is (in a sense we shall discuss more fully later) '*mündig*' or 'come of age', who is Jesus Christ? Is he among those who still acknowledge their need of religion, or is he to be found among those who manifest their *Mündigkeit*, their 'responsible humanity', living *etsi deus non daretur*, as God requires, before God without God. Such persons are not particularly the puzzled religious questioners of Britain in the 1960s; they are just as much the workers he mentions in his christology lectures, not least those who do not even think the question worth bothering with at all. For the question of identity, ours and Christ's, arises with special force in a world where *religious* identity and identifiability can no longer be assumed. Who are you? Christ? Fanatic? Moralist? Market leader? Refugee? Bankrupt? And the response is the question put to us, *Who are we*?

'Today' – the challenge of discernment

Bonhoeffer's christological question appears in the context of a statement about our historical situation. The Christ whom he seeks is a Christ for *today*, and we have the sense that we may read this as meaning that time has some absolute quality, that it exists independently of our values and purposes, and supremely that it exists independently of Christ. A world where the accuracy of a watch with a quartz movement is within the grasp of most people in prosperous societies is a world where we can easily suppose that the more accurately we know the time the more constructively we shall use it.

Yet we also know that the speed with which time passes varies: Christmas seems ages away to our children waiting to unwrap their presents, and all but imminent for parents who have yet to buy them. We know that the couple of minutes it takes the dentist to drill a cavity seems much longer, as do the ten minutes we are kept waiting for an appointment on which a great deal hangs for us. We are aware that whether a speech seems to last a long or a short time depends on many factors other than how many actual minutes it consumes, and that when we are in severe pain just a few minutes can seem an eternity.

Our consciousness has also been greatly affected by an entirely different set of timescales, those of the cosmic history of the universe and of humankind. Alongside our obsession with accuracy to the last second is the knowledge we now have of a massive prehistory that dwarfs our civilisation with its sheer expanse and has to be measured in spans of years that defeat our imagination. Alongside that is the sense of a darker future millions of years hence when the universe is destined to run down and time itself will cease. What has all that to say about our concern to know exactly which second in which minute it is so that we can be sure to fill it?

So time has no absolute status: it measures out our lives not primarily in days and months and years but in what we can do with our days, the past we can remember or would rather forget, and the future we may dread or plan. And whether or not we are religious enough to know that 'the times and seasons are in the Father's hand', we certainly know they are not in ours. Everyone involved in business knows that the least predictable economic reality is timing, and that even if you could be reasonably sure there would be a recovery some day, there are no easy ways to get the timing right, and 'right' means not the right second and minute but the right time in relation to the launching of a new product or the calling of the next election. How or when the teenager who is glad to be thought a year or two older than she is turns into an adult who likes to feel and look young will vary from person to person, but it comes to us all, does it not? Yet even that is determined by aspects of culture that vary greatly from society to society and time to time, and our feelings about ourselves are greatly affected by whether we are surrounded by a cult of youth or of age.

We also need to let ourselves be aware that as well as a culture there is also a *politics* of time. In the absence of constructive and properly rewarded work time hangs heavy upon people; ways to fill it are hard to find and mostly cost money; and the days to the next welfare cheque can seem to last for ever. We know as a matter of experience that who keeps whom waiting – who, that is to say, has time *in* their hands and who is supposed to have time *on* their hands – is a very good indication of where the power lies in a situation. We know that some people get thanked for 'giving up their valuable time', with the clear implication that other people's time is not valuable. We also know very well that such value is not merely an intrinsic or psychological value: 'time is money' we say, knowing that some people's time is better paid than others. We also say that time varies in its quality, and accuse ourselves of not giving our nearest and dearest what we very accurately call 'quality time'.

As well as the natural grain of life, the rhythm of days and seasons, it is a crucial feature of all efforts to produce change, to manipulate the levers of history, that we have to work with the grain of social movements. Ideas have their times when their hour comes; there are historic movements, not always open to us to know or to direct, which determine whether an idea or a programme will simply be confined to the dustbin of human wasted endeavour or will be decisive for the future course of events. The revolutionary developments in Eastern and Central Europe and the recent politics of the United Kingdom, of Eastern Europe and of South Africa are obvious examples of the coming to fruition of ideas that had been around for a long time but whose hour came and was grasped – for better and for worse. In that sense, it is important to say, even ideas whose hour has not come, so far as one can tell, lie there in the store of memory able to be summoned into usefulness when some particular, usually unpredictable, conjunction of events gives them a relevance and a dynamic which really bring about change. The cry, 'How long, O Lord?' is very often the cry of those who are out of time, whose ideas and convictions seem both obviously just and true and, yet evidently destined to be ignored until some unknown future time.

The claim to know what today is, its cultural shape and character, is ultimately a claim to prescribe the framework into which Christ must be fitted. The claim is inevitably patrician: the today that is being referred to is the today of those in power today, those who form the culture of today. Theirs will not be the descriptions of the today of the dispossessed, of those who spend today in terror of their lives or in such pain that they cannot wait for it to end. Such is the fate of all 'todays': to turn out in the end to be the today of those who shape today. That was even true of quite recent attempts to describe the biblical shape of time and to assert that that is the pattern of timekeeping there is for the world. So in his classic *Christ and Time*, Oscar Cullmann writes:

> Our system of reckoning time does not number the years in a continuous forward-moving series that begins at a fixed initial point. That method is followed, for example, in the . . . Jewish calendar, which thinks it possible to fix the date of the creation of the world and . . . simply numbers forward from that point. Our system, however, does not proceed from an initial point, but from a centre; it takes as the mid-point an event which is open to historical investi-

gation and can be chronologically fixed, if not with complete accuracy, at least within a space of a few years. That event is the birth of Jesus Christ of Nazareth. Thence proceed in opposite directions two enumerations, one forward, the other backward: 'after Christ', 'before Christ'.[17]

Such sentiments may embarrass us. They describe a world of Christendom and of massive insensitivity to the desire of Jews and others to have their time, their 'today', taken with full seriousness. Such words read as the assertion of the pre-eminence of the Christian 'today', and claim the calendar for an eternal and exalted Christ. Yet Bonhoeffer's perception of the humiliated God-man is of one whose 'today' is found not with those who control the calendar, not even those who control the calendar allegedly in his name, but with those whose urgencies are treated as of no account.

Such was the today into which Bonhoeffer felt compelled to immerse himself in his famous commendation of life lived fully with God in the world, words which sum up the position he had expounded in his *Ethics*:

[I]t is only by living completely in this world that one learns to have faith. One must completely abandon any attempt to make something of oneself, whether it be a saint, or a converted sinner, or a churchman. . . . By this-worldliness I mean living unreservedly in life's duties, problems, successes and failures, experiences and perplexities. In so doing we throw ourselves completely into the arms of God, taking seriously not our own sufferings, but those of God in the world – watching with Christ in Gethsemane.[18]

Thus the 'today' of Bonhoeffer's question can be read in liberal or radical mode: it may be the today of those who are sure of their own today and ask how Christ may fit into it, or it may be that 'today' may be today as Christ the 'humiliated God-man' sees it and asks us to see it. On the one hand we may see today from the perspective of an old world perplexed as to whether Christ can be understood today, or we may seek to see it from the viewpoint of those whose today is that of the humiliated one whose perspective on today is of no account. Among those we must of course include generations yet unborn, who have no voice in decisions about how our world is to be used and abused in the service of those who rule, and shape, our 'today'.

'Us' – the challenge of solidarity

The preacher's text, 'If God is for us, who is against us?' (Romans 8:31), could have led in a number of directions at an ordination; but this preacher, Bishop Simon Phipps, chose to present the Christian life, and Christian priesthood, as having above all to do with the meaning of 'us'.[19] He began with an account of an event portrayed on television: an aircraft had crashed into the sea, though remaining watertight. When one of the crew offered to leave through a hatch and attempt to surface with a transmitter, a passenger who was an experienced diver offered to go with him. His wife remonstrated with him, but he responded, 'It's for the good of all of us.' That prompted the very human reply, 'Us? Who's "us"? *We're* us. This is just a bunch of strangers.'

'Who's "us"?' is neither an elegant nor even a grammatical question. I distinguish it from the other question, 'Who are we?', as that question asks for characterisation, for a statement of identity such as we were considering in an earlier section. As such it can be a very profound question; but it is not the one with which we are concerned here. For the question of 'us' is the issue of the boundaries of our solidarity, the territory beyond which all we see is 'just a bunch of strangers'.

Bonhoeffer's resistance to Hitler and the persecution of the Jews is sufficiently well known for me not to elaborate on the obvious relevance of Bonhoeffer's life and thought to the issue of 'Who's "us"?', or of the implications and inspiration derived from his courage by those resisting racist ideologies. Propelled as he was into many of the positions that he took by an ideology of race which proved singularly attractive to the majority of his Christian fellow citizens, he has been an obvious person to call in aid for those seeking in the name of Christ to confront such ideologies in the intervening decades. John de Gruchy has both led and chronicled the relationship of a theological dialogue with Bonhoeffer and the political resistance to apartheid in South Africa,[20] and quite apart from the analogy with Nazism we know of the extent to which Bonhoeffer himself was moved by the situation of Black Americans during his time in New York.[21] In the context of the nationalisms of our time, writers such as Keith Clements have had resort to him in the search for a true patriotism.[22]

Christ's refusal to accommodate to any self-chosen 'us', and his demand that the identity of any 'us' should be the one that appears in the light of him alone, remains a pressing issue. Naturally it is not usually a matter of controversy among believers that in theory human rights should be accorded to all citizens irrespective of ethnic origin. That level of understanding may carry weight within the life of the nation-state. But its inadequacy becomes evident when we consider the increasing number of people who are driven from their homelands by the pressures of war and oppression and are left to beg for rights of abode and sustenance from other nations which retain their right to determine who comprise 'us'. In a European context there is no sign of any fundamental questioning of the right of human communities to decide the boundaries of their solidarity and the identity of their 'us'.

It is not hard to see what are the politics of the current determination in many countries, not least the United Kingdom, to 'tighten up' on immigration procedures, under the guise of barring the door to 'bogus asylum-seekers'. The weasel words whereby the object of such proposals is to 'safeguard community relations' cannot conceal the fact that when legislation is introduced which assumes that asylum-seekers are likely to be liars there is a clear implication about all recent arrivals in European countries that they were probably liars too. To give as one of the answers to Bonhoeffer's question that Jesus Christ for us today is a *refugee* is not after all to say anything that is not clearly rooted in the Gospel of Matthew. Any political judgement about the power of the nation-state to administer its borders must at some point come face to face with the claim of Christ to a decisive voice in the matter of deciding who 'us' is.

Yet in seeking to honour Bonhoeffer's legacy we cannot only take up the points where there are obvious parallels between the issues we face and the racism he found it necessary to resist. It is precisely the areas of our current political situation which he does *not* appear to address which we may need to take up. In a world in which nationalisms and ethnic division continue to be occasions of hatred and bloodshed it may seem almost bizarre to suggest that there are other ways in which the issue of boundaries to our solidarity – the question, *Who's 'us'?* – are arising, and which are more sinister and hold yet more menace for the future of humankind.

Let us return to the meeting in a Bulawayo hotel to which I referred earlier. The message to that meeting, together with a host of other pieces of evidence, makes it clear to us that the ideology of racism can be opposed by the instruments of the marketplace. (In noticing that, however, we must never forget the role of those who put their lives on the line in a far more direct way than those who only abstained from eating South African oranges.) In the end it was surely clear that the prosperity even of those who were enjoying it would not be able to continue unless apartheid were dismantled.

Yet I believe there is a profoundly sinister aspect to that development. We were all assured that the trends in the world economy were all ultimately beneficial, provided unnecessary and old-fashioned restrictions could be removed. The world was moving, we were told, in the direction of a free market, of low taxation, of the exportability of capital and knowhow. Is such a world one in which the challenge of 'Who's "us"?' would finally have been answered? Or is it not rather a world in which the power to decide who 'us' is has been handed over to those who have the capacity to succeed in the market, and ultimately to control it?

It is here, surely, that we come up against Bonhoeffer's fundamental stance in his approach to the question of who Jesus Christ is for us today. In his critique of Bultmann in the letter of 5 May 1944, he calls Bultmann's approach 'still a liberal one (i.e. abridging the gospel)' in contrast to his own which is 'trying to think theologically'.[23] That is, the question of who Jesus Christ is for us today cannot be interpreted so as to mean that we know who 'us' is and that the question is therefore how Jesus Christ is somehow to be accommodated to that 'us'. Rather, to use the language of the Barcelona address, if Jesus Christ is to have something decisive to say about the deepest decisions we have to take concerning us and our people, he has to be able to be decisive precisely about who the 'us' is.

In contrast to what 'thinking theologically' must mean, the attraction of the market is that it appears to offer a method for deciding who 'us' is apart from Christ. It is a response not to the question who 'us' is, but to its own quite different question: what is the best method for deciding who is of 'us' and who is not (that is to say principally, who shall inherit the riches of the earth and who shall not)? We seem here to have precisely what Bonhoeffer means by the 'godless question, the question of the serpent', which supplants the 'transcendent' question of who Christ is for us with the 'immanent' question of *how* Christ is for us, the question by which Christ cannot ever be grasped. We are reminded here very directly of the lawyer's question. 'Who is my neighbour?' (by which he meant, of course, 'Who am I free to regard as *not* my neighbour?'), to which the only possible response was a story that raised an entirely different question.

If the question 'Who is Jesus Christ for us today?' is to be addressed, therefore, it has to be on the basis that Jesus Christ is not the one who accommodates himself to prior decisions, reached predominantly through the instrument of the market, about who 'us' is, but on the basis that only in and through him is the decision about the boundaries of our solidarity to be made. When we know him we know who 'us' is, and without submitting our decisions about who 'us' is to him we shall not know who he is.

In this connection I think it most important that we address the context that Bonhoeffer was considering in raising the question of who Jesus Christ is for us today. His concern is with Christ and the world come of age. This *Mündigkeit* he explicates in terms of the end of the religious *a priori*, of humanity's accountability for itself and of the end of the 'alibi' of God. He sees that as a historical development, and a benign one. In its English translation, 'adulthood', it is not surprising that *Mündigkeit* should be seen as the result of a progressive human self-emancipation, a process as irrevocable as is the growing up of an individual person.

Yet the metaphor of *Mündigkeit* makes a more profound point. Its reference is to the point where someone is a legally responsible person, able to speak for herself and enter into obligations on her own account. In most cases, of course, that point is arrived at through the passing of years, when a person reaches the age of majority and is no longer regarded as, to use the Latin metaphor 'in-fant', unable to speak. But there are categories besides the young who are denied the right to speak for themselves: the imprisoned and those certified as insane, not to mention the whole list of *Unmenschen*, non-persons who were the creation of the Third Reich – and not just of the Third Reich.

Once we remove the connotations of inevitability and irrevocability from our perception of the human situation in the modern era, the language of a world 'come of age' can hold out, in a contemporary reading and appropriation of the legacy of Dietrich Bonhoeffer, a vision that is both realistic and challenging. We shall not be naïvely blind to the possibility that people, societies and communities will be put back 'under guardianship' willingly or unwillingly, deprived of autonomy and the right to act responsibly, *entmündigt*, put under administration, reduced to a level at which their own decisions count for nothing. Thus understood, the high cost and the tremendous fragility of the declaration that the world is *mündig geworden*, 'come of age', come very quickly and clearly before our eyes, as does the great difficulty which human beings have in bearing that reality.

In particular, the claim of the market to be a symbol of human freedom and responsibility comes under the judgement of all those who are restricted and bound, *entmündigt*, by its operation: how else can we describe the nations of the Two-Thirds World, whose indebtedness and whose structural adjustment programmes, forced upon them, we shall discuss in a later chapter? How else are we to regard the individuals and the whole communities within the world's more prosperous societies for whom the market is neither the symbol of nor the key to their freedom, but the means by which they are reduced, as all debtors in history have been reduced, to incapacity and ultimately to effective slavery? Most serious of all is the fact that since what happens to them is made to appear to come about through the operation of the 'free market' there is added to the injury of their overwhelming poverty the insult of the conviction that they themselves are to blame.

So it is that Bonhoeffer's question, and ours, about who Christ is for us today, leads us to engage with the market and its claims. We shall need to assert, for our time, the unique right of Christ to the definition of 'us', and that means refusing that right to institutions in society, however useful they may seem to be for certain purposes. It is true that in the case of South Africa the operation of the market seems to have been a useful instrument for ending the power of a racist state; and it would seem that the efficiency of the market compared with centralised command economies has played its part in the downfall of communist regimes. But we still need to see how the market too has the capacity to offer itself as idol, as alternative 'Christ', asserting its own claim and creating its own 'us' and its own 'bunch of strangers'. Thus the question of who Christ is for us today turns out to have more to do with his claim for obedience from us than with our perplexity about his relevance to us.

Conclusion: Christ and our whole image

I have sought to demonstrate in this chapter that Bonhoeffer's writing and his life offer more to the exploration of a contemporary way of speaking about Christ than an epigrammatic question, though it was that question which certainly set me on this road. The language of the question itself offered us key issues with which Bonhoeffer had to engage and which we in our time must also engage. For he links the task of speaking of Jesus as the Christ in our time to the critical matters of identity, of discernment and of solidarity, and in so doing shows that the question of Christ holds up a mirror to those who ask it.

At the same time Bonhoeffer holds before us two criteria which need to be applied to statements about Jesus Christ: they must speak in language that has not been co-opted into the exclusive realm of religion, speaking to humanity, that is to say, in individualistic and inward ways; contact must be re-established between the language about Christ and the language of the world about us and its realities. Secondly, it must address humanity in its strength, not relying on a sense of alienation or weakness to gain a spurious purchase on human life but both appreciating and confronting a humanity come to maturity, answerable for itself and not dependent on religion for either survival or explanation. That exploration, those questions and those criteria have brought us to the place where Christ is quite literally in the marketplace; for that is the place where human *Mündigkeit* is supremely making itself felt, and with whose realities we shall have to struggle if Christ is to be spoken of today.

But there is also a further inner tension, of which I have

become even more strongly aware even in the process of this exploration. On the one hand I am the product of a liberal theological culture as a result of which I first heard the question, 'Who is Jesus Christ for us today?' The perplexity which that gave me about how Christ might be understood and related to my world of today remains, and the climate in which the question has to be faced is if anything more hostile than when I first heard it.

At the same time, I hear Bonhoeffer, whom I have got to know more closely since I heard that question express my perplexity, speak with a different voice. It is a voice which seems to me to be the authentic bearer of the Christian vocation to discipleship, and a witness to a Christ who (as the title Christ implies) continues to make the decisive claim expressed in the Barcelona address. He continues to make it, furthermore, not with the force of state coercion or the power of the market-leader, but as the humiliated God-man.

As such he is uniquely able to tell us about our 'today' for he has dined with those who have had no part in shaping the culture out of which we voice our perplexity. As such he can ask us about the boundaries of our 'us' because he has lived and died outside them. As such he is able to turn our question to him, 'Who are you for us today?' into his question, 'Who are you?'

This is indeed a new day, and not just for our own society. The new day brings new perplexities in the form of issues about democracy, about the economy, about the vision of humanity, in short, that informs our common life. Among those who face the new day will be those who have a question and a perplexity about the identity of Christianity, and indeed of Christ himself, in our time. In Dietrich Bonhoeffer we have someone who was both close enough to his own culture to feel its perplexity in the face of its coming of age, and yet sure enough of the claim of the Christ among the excluded of his time to be a disciple. Sometimes tensions paralyse us, and in particular cause us not to see the possibilities of a new day. Sometimes, however, we need the determination to hear two voices clearly, the voice of the culture that has given us our questions and the voice of those who have no part in that culture. That, I am suggesting, is probably the only way we shall be able to speak authentically of Christ in our time.

We have reached the point where we must turn to that feature of life in our time to which I have already referred on a number of occasions, and which is so dominant: the world of credit and debt, and of the market which has increased in size both absolutely and relatively in our generation, and which shows no sign of losing either its impetus to grow or its power in the lives of people. If Christ is to be spoken of in our time it must be in relation to that reality and, as we shall see, not only in relation to those debtors who are rendered weak and helpless by it, but also to those who derive their power and wealth as creditors within it. As we shall see later, this may be a factor of particular dominance in our age; but it is by no means a new one – others seeking to speak of faith in Christ have confronted it before.

A mountain to move

As a nation we have thrown away the piggy bank on the mantelpiece and now rely on future income to buy what we want today.

As we shall see in this review, this has not been a painless process. There have been, and still are, serious consumer casualties on the road to financial sophistication.[1]

The outline of an explosion

Such is the gentle comment with which the National Consumer Council introduces its 1990 review of credit and debt in the United Kingdom. Gentle it certainly is, given the context of an increase in consumer debt during the ten years from 1980 from around £11 billion to around £43 billion, while mortgage borrowing increased more than fivefold, and by the end of the 1980s stood at £300 billion.[2]

During the month of January 1995 the total of credit card purchases in shops came to £5.3 billion pounds, that is to say an average of around £100 for every man, woman and child in the United Kingdom. This spending was no doubt a source of considerable delight to retailers and credit card operators alike, and was hailed by politicians looking for signs of economic recovery. Naturally a large proportion of credit card use is not seen as credit at all, but is simply seen as a convenient way of paying, the balance being paid off without interest when it appears on the customer's statement; nevertheless that 'interest-free' period does represent a debt which has to be financed by the retailers through the commission they pay to the credit card companies, and is therefore still part of the total picture of indebtedness.

As we should expect, there are marked differences in the use of credit according to people's income levels; so it perhaps comes as no surprise that the use of credit is almost universal among members of the highest income group. What is a more serious reflection of the rapid changes in the profile of indebtedness is the situation as it affected members of the lowest income group, among whom the decade saw an increase in the use of credit from 22 per cent to 69 per cent. Participation in the culture of credit and debt is now for practical purposes an index of participation in society at all; even the social fund, which replaced emergency grants to those in receipt of family credit, can be seen as a way of integrating claimants, the poorest members of our society, into the credit economy. Students similarly receive an education with their loan: not just the education for which their fees are paying, but an education in the acceptance of debt and credit as a normal part of human existence, a view encouraged not just by the existence of student loans but by the blandishment of 'free' overdrafts by the banks, in the hope that their new customers will turn on graduation into interest-paying borrowers.

In such a situation of rapid credit growth it is hardly surprising that the number of those for whom indebtedness has become a problem has grown too. One of the key figures cited in Wolfe's *Handbook of Debt Advice* is the number of those asking for help from the Citizens' Advice Bureaux. The total of those seeking advice over problems of indebtedness doubled between 1980 and 1989, and doubled again in the period from 1989 to 1995.[3] More serious still is the fact that in the first two months of 1992 alone 280,000 personal debtors applied to be made bankrupt, a record, and almost 80 per cent more than in the same months of 1991.

A further group with indebtedness problems is those who have loans secured on their homes. Here too the growth in the use of this form of credit has had the inevitable by-product of a vast increase in the numbers in arrears with their payments. In the period of the 1980s when, as has been said, mortgage debt increased fivefold, the increase in those in arrears by between six and twelve months grew far faster: from 13,500 in 1980 to 183,610 in 1991, with another half a million with less serious arrears.[4] Those whose arrears were so serious that their homes were repossessed increased in number twenty-fivefold in the same period, from 3000 to more than 75,000. Since a good deal of publicity accompanied arrangements made by mortgage lenders, with government encouragement, to reduce the number of repossessions, it is worth noticing that more than 25,000 homes were repossessed in the first half of 1995, itself an increase of 4 per cent on the same period the previous year.

Although these bare figures are dramatic enough, we shall need to return to some of the 'losers' in the credit explosion later; their plight has been analysed from numerous standpoints and with great care. There has also been no lack of remedies offered for those in difficulties: sources of advice have grown, and more lenders have sought to make provision for those whose indebtedness has become a problem to them (and, at least as significantly, to their lenders too). Nevertheless, the increased number of those who have got into difficulties through debt has not really dented the confidence of who see the credit explosion as a basic good, productive of prosperity and conducive to the well-being of us all. We shall need to keep this basically optimistic consensus very much in mind if we are to take seriously Bonhoeffer's theological challenge to discover ways of addressing humanity in its strength and success, and not only to care for cases of weakness.

'Forget it for an instant'

The move which is described by the National Consumer Council as away 'from the piggy bank', and one which Wolfe describes as the 'transformation of "confidential easy terms" into "instant credit" ', is bound also to reflect a massive change in public opinion on the acceptability of credit and debt. A nearly fourfold increase in indebtedness could hardly have been accomplished without such a massive shift, a cultural earthquake which appears not just in the numbers of people experiencing severe problems with indebtedness but in public attitudes generally, which show a marked change from those of a previous generation. Whether 'financial sophistication' is the best description to apply to that change, or at least whether in this aspect of life sophistication is to be welcomed, is something we shall have to consider. After all, it is not more than a generation ago that it would have been generally felt wise and public-spirited to pay off your mortgage loan early if you could, so as to avoid being in unnecessary debt and to make it possible for others who needed to borrow the

money for house purchase to do so; a person approaching their
building society now about early repayment on those grounds
would be rewarded at best with the benign smile reserved for
those who have not 'moved with the times' and at worst with a
warning of the severe financial penalty that such early repayments
incur.

Some of the optimism about the ready availability of credit
may have taken a knock. We may suspect that more people have
reservations about it now than had a few years ago; but none
the less the expansion in the financial services industry and the
increase in the number of pages of daily and Sunday newspapers
devoted to the better management of your money suggest that
making more money from your money has become one of the
subjects in which the public appetite for information continues
to grow at great speed.

One of the great attractions of the subject of money for
producers of literature and advice is the happy and widespread
thought that in this aspect of life all can be winners. If there are
losers as a result of clever dealing in money, they are for the
most part invisible. If they become visible, because they experience debt problems or their house is repossessed, that can easily
be represented as the result of foolishness on their part or on the
part of those who should have advised them better, or else simply
as bad luck; if we are in a position to make money out of the
money we already have we generally do not need to trouble
ourselves with the thought that our gains were at anyone else's
expense. Whether that very convenient assumption is in fact
justified is a question to which we shall have to return.

Certainly we have lived through an enormous credit
explosion, and even without a detailed examination of the
figures, many would feel that what the National Consumer
Council had to say in its 1980 report sounds like a voice from
the rather distant past:

> The general message of our work has been reassuring. We
> found no evidence of widespread serious credit problems,
> and a wide choice of credit generally available to people.
> People generally manage to get the sort of credit they want,
> and it is rare for them to be dissatisfied with it once they
> have got it.

Not surprisingly therefore, the Council was able to be quite mild in its recommendations, and its language in making them certainly reflects the confident free market rhetoric of the time:

> In general, as far as lenders and credit operators are concerned, we see more advantage in co-operation and persuasion than in rigid regulatory coercion; for most borrowers, educated self-help rather than cosseting.[5]

The Council's rather less happy 1990 report is important in highlighting the fact that trends in the credit market do not necessarily reflect what a rational consideration of the state of the economy would suggest. So it is not too difficult to account for the fact that demand for credit grew during the 1970s when inflation was high and access to credit still relatively limited. That gave support to the view that it was better to be a borrower than a lender, that it was financially prudent to buy now and pay later. These same factors in the economy would be expected to, and did, depress the savings market and cause the raising of interest rates to be a much-used instrument of financial regulation by the government.

What might seem more puzzling is that during the 1980s, when inflation was falling and personal disposable income for those in work was rising rapidly, credit expanded rapidly and savings similarly declined. Despite the fact that people had more money to spend than before, with real personal disposable income increasing by almost 8 per cent in the two years from 1986 to 1988, and even though the inflationary pressures of the late seventies and early eighties were easing, people were not saving. Indeed consumption grew 25 per cent faster than the gross national product. Clearly the experience of those in work that they had more to spend led to their deciding to consume more and finance their consumption by a rapid increase in borrowing. People did not seem ready to discard the lessons of the 1970s even when economists thought they safely could.

At the same time, there has been a huge change in the way in which credit is make available to those who desire it. The single most powerful statistic in this respect is that the number of credit cards increased from eight to twenty-five million in the decade from 1978 to 1988, and in the five years from 1980 outstanding credit on cards increased by 30 per cent per year. Although this slowed down in the later years of the last decade, the fact that the outstanding amount was still growing at the rate of 11 per cent per year shows that the momentum of credit growth is still there.

Although there are signs of a wider concern about levels of indebtedness, therefore, we have to assume that without a radical consideration of the character and effects of credit and debt, and a willingness to control its growth by the kind of action on the part of government of which there is currently no hint, most people are at worst resigned and at best delighted at the thought of seeing a critical role for credit and debt into the future. We shall look in more detail at the components of this apparently inexorable growth. It is as well to begin with the form of credit that is least challenged and that has become in our society most unavoidable: housing debt – or, in most people's parlance, 'the mortgage'.

Millstones and mortar

Last summer, Mr Ian Campbell Forbes, an intelligent businessman in his mid-40's, found himself living in the hut which in happier days had been the home of the family's pet rabbit. His wife Yvonne was being put up by kindly neighbours, while their teenage sons James and George occupied a tent in their friend's garden down the road.[6]

There are various ways of assessing the social importance of mortgage debt. For example, we can consider the rise in home ownership, the vast majority of which is financed by mortgage loans: looked at in that way, the rise is dramatic – in the half century from the outbreak of the 1914–18 war, the proportion of households owning their own home rose from a tenth to more than a half; a decade and a half later, in 1980, the proportion was 56.2 per cent; five years on, in 1985, it was up to nearly 62 per cent, and there is no sign of the growth slowing down.[7]

Another way of assessing the social importance of a phenomenon, however, is the amount of academic and other interest in research into the problems which it is generating. It is instructive to note how far the subject of mortgage arrears has moved from being one about which a researcher in 1978 could say, 'There is so little information about mortgage arrears that it is hard to pin down the extent of the problem, let alone define the causes';[8] in that year the same writer referred to mortgage arrears as providing 'tomorrow's problems'.[9] By the mid-1980s, however, there was already a huge literature about the subject,[10] while at a more popular level, radio and television coverage of the problems of arrears and the incidence of repossession was such that politicians felt a need to be seen taking initiatives to deal with the problem.

There is no doubt that 'owning your own home' has a natural appeal which makes it seem preferable to other forms of tenure, even in circumstances where there are rational arguments against it. Being able to call the bricks and mortar that shelter you 'your own' gives a feeling of security that often gets in the way of serious reflection on the responsibilities and risks involved. Indeed, until the prices of houses fell sharply at the end of the eighties, most regarded house purchase as an almost risk-free form of investment, whose tangible quality and structural solidity exuded a sense of permanence quite unlike figures on a bank statement or names on share certificates. All political parties have been agreed in regarding the home-owning constituency as crucial to their success, and have needed a good deal of pressure before they would be seen to question a situation in which natural preferences are supported by deliberately engineered financial advantages: income tax relief on mortgage interest is, as its name suggests, able to be seen as 'relief', which is a good thing. On the other hand assisted tenancies of one kind or another, particularly in the local authority sector, continue to be described as 'subsidised', which received wisdom has it is a bad thing.

This has been a strong feature of the housing policies of the 1980s, with the Housing Act of 1980 offering large incentives to tenants of local authorities and many housing associations to become owner-occupiers and a right to a local authority mortgage loan. In fact most of the purchases did not require local authority finance, because the government was simultaneously deregulating credit in general and the operation of the building societies in particular, to such an extent that the shortage of money for mortgage lending, which had been characteristic of earlier decades, was replaced by eager competition among building societies, joined now by the banks, to lend as much as possible. Between 1970 and 1985 the annual number of mortgage loans increased by more than 80 per cent, while the amount lent on mortgage increased by an incredible twelve and a half times.

It is worth noting the kind of language that is used to describe these events: the days when mortgages were hard to come by are usually described as the time of 'mortgage queues' and 'mortgage rationing', words which conjure up images of wartime food shortages or the empty supermarket shelves in the former command economies of Eastern Europe. It has taken the harsh experience of the late 1980s and early 1990s when house prices fell dramatically to enable some at least to notice that it may have been precisely the over-availability of credit that was largely responsible for the massive increase in house prices on which they had previously relied; even so, that period of massive fluctuation is generally spoken of as a regrettable hiccup in an otherwise entirely benign set of developments, a cautionary tale suggesting the need for taking care about the speed of change rather than requiring any questioning of its basic direction.

Yet while houses may project an image of permanence and security, the financial aspects of home ownership have come for many to present a less comforting picture. It is, after all, not just the bricks and mortar that have to be secure, but the income of the occupants also. Even the bricks and mortar, however, make their own financial demands. In their survey of the diversity of experience of home ownership, Doling and Stafford uncover evidence of the effect of home ownership on the priorities in people's expenditure on their home: not surprisingly, if your house is thought of as something to sell rather than as a place to live, then what you do to its fabric will be affected by market considerations.[11] If there is spare money it is likely to be spent on improvements that would be attractive to a potential purchaser, rather than on running repairs; much publicity has been given to those who purchased their council flats only to find that the costs of structural repairs and redecoration vastly exceeded their expectations.

It is also understandable that those who see their house as something they are likely to sell will if possible delay repairs until the point of sale, hoping that the expected rise in the monetary value of their house will more than compensate them for any reduction in the price that may be negotiated on account of the poor state of repair. Repairs that are not carried out are thus in effect a further loan, repayable in the future out of capital rather than out of current income. This particular tendency is a by-product of home ownership which may be doing little good to the quality of the nation's housing stock, and of course becomes a further reason why any fall in house prices generally has such severe consequences for borrowers. We should not be surprised by the conclusion of a recent piece of research into mortgage arrears that

> For many households, the need for repairs and improvements to their property and the financial outlay necessary is a major contributing factor to the development of arrears. . . . A substantial proportion of the people involved in this study have remortgaged their properties or have taken on additional loans to cover the costs of repairs or improvements to their properties.[12]

Thus one loan is needed to support another, and the 'most secure investment of all' becomes a major source of further indebtedness.

Much more serious, however, is the fact that the sense of physical security provided by house ownership will certainly prove to be an illusion if the owner falls victim to one of the many other insecurities which have become more and more pronounced even as home ownership has been extended. At a time when employment is uncertain, and in particular when the average length of periods out of work has increased dramatically (even if total unemployment shows signs of falling), mortgage repayments are a long-term commitment which can have very serious consequences at a time when stability of income is much less assured.

At the same time as unemployment rose, so did the public encouragement of people to start their own businesses. Such self-employment may be the right course for particular individuals, but is almost certain to involve two consequences which will be of particular importance in relation to the debt they owe on their property. First, self-employment is likely to mean that income will fluctuate and will not be assured; and secondly, the need to capitalise the business will almost certainly involve borrowing money from the bank, which in its turn is very likely to require a second charge on the borrower's home. Failure of the business therefore places in jeopardy not just income but the home as well.

The other stabilities that gave a sense of security to the family home are similarly under threat for increasing numbers of people. In their description of the context within which the increase in property ownership has occurred Doling, Ford and Stafford, while regarding the changes in the labour market as the most significant factor of all, particularly refer to the increased instability in relationships:

The last ten years or so have seen fundamental changes in the fabric of British society. . . . Since the beginning of the 1970s the pace of marital breakdown has quickened; about one in three marriages now ends in divorce. Unmarried couples are increasingly setting up household together and the household consisting of man, wife and children is no longer the norm.[13]

In her study of credit and default in the 1980s, Janet Ford tells numerous stories of the effect of relationship breakdown on a couple's capacity to discharge its obligations to a building society. While she makes the point that the connection is not necessarily a simple one of cause and effect, these two aspects of life, the unstable relationship and the increasing indebtedness, interact with each other in a variety of ways.[14] The pattern of building society loans for house purchase evolved at a time when social stability of a kind we have ceased to be able to take for granted was assumed, and where breakdowns in relationships could be seen as exceptional. Such a change of context is likely to mean that the shared relationship and shared commitment to a long-term debt move from being mutually reinforcing aspects of a total climate of stability to being competing claims and mutually aggravating difficulties.

The total picture of mortgage debt is thus one in which conflicting messages for those who set up house at the present time pull them in different directions:

The combination of all these changes has resulted in a situation where, on the one hand, more people than ever before are buying their homes and, on the other hand, many social and economic changes are undermining the sort of stability which is consistent with the long term financial commitment of taking on a mortgage. Arguably our system of housing has been shifting away from public provision based on need as the criterion for allocation towards market provision based on the willingness and ability to pay, during a period when the willingness and ability to pay is being undermined by other changes in society.[15]

Many who would acknowledge the difficulties some have experienced through housing debt would still say that I have in this account, like the researchers on whose work it is based, presented far too bleak a picture: that many of those who bought their council houses, and many other participants in the housing market, have found the experience of home ownership liberating; that they have felt free to make decisions about their housing without needing the agreement of their local authority; and that they have been willing therefore to improve their living environment according to their own taste, knowing that there was a reasonable chance that they might recover their expenditure because the asset was their own.

I do not doubt that these positive experiences are there for large numbers of people, and even that many who have had difficulties would still not wish to return to being council tenants: home ownership does indeed produce, as Doling and Stafford state, 'a variety of experience'. What has happened, however, and all the research has tended to this conclusion, is the establishment of home ownership, and therefore mortgage debt, as the norm to which all should aspire. As a result, and through the withering away of other forms of tenure, many have been drawn into a level of indebtedness and a length of commitment well beyond their means; those able to undertake and to enjoy undertaking such commitments thus set a standard for the society as a whole which may be quite inappropriate to those who are then drawn into it. It is the establishment of mortgage debt as a *norm* that determines the life choices of those who then find, too late, that for them it is a road to disaster. The establishment of ownership as the normative form of tenure means in effect the establishment of a society living on a mountain of debt. And as is the case with mountains, some climbers upon them are in a position to admire the view from the top, while others fall victim to the rocky climb or insufficient oxygen, or fall into an unforeseen crevasse. And if such a picture fails to convey the distress that goes with losing your home because it has become impossible to keep up the payments, it is only necessary to enter a house or a flat that has been repossessed to feel the shame and anger almost palpably emerging from the walls – and then to reflect that in 1991 alone the number of people who suffered that indignity was more than the entire population of Southampton.

'Take the waiting out of wanting'

The highly successful slogan with which Access launched its credit card touches a very raw nerve. Nobody is without the experience of wanting something they could not yet have, or the frustrating experience of waiting for an uncertain length of time for something which they have come to believe they want, or need, or deserve. In our reflection on Bonhoeffer's question, the word 'today' figured prominently, and it is arguable that the largest change in the credit and debt scene has precisely to do with the requirement to have things 'today', combined with the possibility of doing so.

In its most obvious sense, consumer credit is a device for enabling consumers to have what they want sooner, to gain the benefit now of the income they expect to have in the future. But there is another sense also in which the changes in the credit market are also about the shortening of timescale, for *obtaining* credit is now a very speedy matter. Although credit is still made available by individual agreement for the purchase of large items such as cars, electrical goods, double-glazing or major pieces of furniture, the main source of increased lending has come through forms of credit that do not require individual negotiation before being taken up. The trebling within a decade of the number of credit cards in use has already been mentioned: to that must be added the enormous competition in the offering of personal loans and second mortgages. It is a feature of such lending that no discussion is required about the purpose of the loan; it is a facility granted on the security either of the borrower's future income or, in the case of second mortgages, of their property.

In the case of personal loans, there is a particular attraction to 'becoming a cash buyer', a person able to write out a cheque for a large amount without the seller needing to know that the money is borrowed; in the case of credit cards there need be no charge or inconvenience to having the facility simply to go into a shop and sign for anything you want. There is a sense here of having been admitted to what used to be the very select club of people who 'had an account' at a shop and could simply sign for their goods. 'Sign for it and take it away' is the attractive opportunity available to all 'credit-worthy' people: not only can you have today what you might have had to save up for over a long period, but the whole process can be completed in the time it takes to sign your name and to check your credentials on a dedicated phone line.

The store account also has attained new levels of sophistication: in exchange for a regular monthly payment customers may purchase goods for, say, thirty or more times this amount. Once the facility has been granted, not only can it be used for any products sold in the store, but the credit is constantly being topped up as the monthly payments are recorded. In this way, not to have purchased items up to the limit of your available credit comes to feel like neglecting an opportunity; after all, what was the point of opening the credit account if you do not use it?

It is important to notice here other advantages, from the lenders' and sellers' points of view, of an extension of the use of credit. It is clear that one of the things that has enabled this vast expansion is the exponential growth in information technology: the swift availability and authorisation of loans has happened in part because of new possibilities opened up by the computer age. It has not taken long for other advantages to become apparent. For instance, a lender has a record of all the transactions made with each individual and is easily able to compile a profile of each person's expected needs and of the products likely to arouse their interest. We are accustomed to advertisements in newspapers or in literature that comes through the door offering us enticing items to buy. This is a somewhat random process, however; would it not be a huge saving of expense if advertising information could be made available at the right time and only to the right people? This is precisely what is rendered possible by the combination of a highly sophisticated credit market and the computer recording of transactions. If you buy a washing machine on credit it will be simplicity itself for the seller to make sure that you receive information about up-to-date models at the time when it may be expected that yours is beginning to wear out or starting to look and feel rather old.

The relationship of creditor and debtor exacts a price for the foreshortening of timescale which it offers. You can indeed have today what you might otherwise only be able to have next year, and you can indeed have in seconds the loan which replaces the 'easy terms' which previously took a rather uncomfortable interview with the shop manager, or obtain through the post a personal loan from your bank which earlier required a lengthy conversation with your bank manager. But the process also creates a bond – it is a word we must not take lightly – which is rendered the more effective by being recorded on a computerised record, enabling the lender or seller to increase your vulnerability to further offers and to keep a careful record of your preferences. We should not suppose either that this process of acquiring information about buyers and borrowers occurs only among those with relatively high incomes: among those who buy from mail-order catalogues – a method of purchase on credit where the amount of interest (usually described as 'free') is concealed in the price – there is also a system of revolving credit, enabling the company to draw on the 'loyalty' of its customers, encouraging them to spend up to their credit limit, and in the process to give the lenders a detailed profile of their expenditure pattern.

Even this broad description of the implications of the expansion of credit does not give an adequate impression. For to the additional knowledge of buyers and borrowers which lenders and sellers gain must be added the fact that such knowledge is increasingly shared among lenders through the highly centralised system of credit scoring which is almost universally employed by them.[16] Banks, building societies, public utilities and mail-order firms now use the services of the two major credit bureaux and find that such sharing of information in the form of credit scores is highly successful, and to be preferred in every way to the use of their own staffs' subjective judgements.

It might be argued that a system that prevents lenders from incurring bad debts is also in the interests of borrowers, protecting them from undertaking commitments which are beyond their capacity to manage. But in his discussion of the matter, Lyn Thomas offers two important provisos: the first has to do with the status and quality of the information that is recorded; and the second with the overall effect of such a system on the character of the market for credit.

As to the status of the information, he makes a number of

points. In the absence of legal regulation other than the slight
protection afforded by the Data Protection and Consumer Credit
Acts, there is little control over what is recorded and how what
is recorded is used in the scoring process. The information is
likely also to be out of date, perhaps by two or three years, and
this is of particular importance given the evidence that much
default derives from sudden changes in people's personal circumstances – illness, redundancy or sudden items of unforeseen
expenditure.

It is however the second implication of the rise in the use of
'instant' credit to which Thomas refers that holds the greater
threat. What has emerged in effect is a double market in credit:
there are those who borrow by means which are instant and
impersonal; and there are those who borrow without having
credit cards or the other apparatus of immediate loans. To make
the point, Thomas undertook a comparison between the 1987
and 1991 Family Expenditure Surveys published by the Central
Statistical Office. These analyse a fortnight's expenditure by
between 12,500 and 13,500 people, and include information on
the proportion holding credit cards. What the comparison shows
is that while the proportion of the population using some form
of credit had not increased significantly during that period, there
had been a marked shift towards the use of credit cards. This
shift occurred just as much among house owners as among those
who rented, and just as much among the waged as among
those living on benefits. The proportions of such groups holding
credit cards would of course differ, but in each case the use
of credit showed a marked swing towards the use of credit cards.

There are thus two kinds of market in credit: the instant and
the 'traditional', with those who lack credit cards being thereby
less able to use their kind of instant credit with its advantages of
convenience and speed. This in turn means that the trends
reinforce themselves: as more and more people have credit cards
and thereby acquire a credit score, so *not* having such a card
exacts more and more of a penalty in the form of exclusion from
the world of easy credit. We have certainly reached the point
where if you think you are ever likely to need credit you should
avail yourself of a credit card so that you can acquire a good
credit score. Credit is supremely an area of life where 'to those
who have will be given; and from those who have not even
what they have will be taken away.'

This brings us directly to the question of attitudes to credit and debt: is there a distinction between these and if so what does the distinction represent in terms of people's willingness to 'accept' credit or 'incur' debt? Is it simply that debts are what 'other people' get into, whereas credit is what *I* enjoy – and deserve? If we may suppose that such a vast expansion in the amount consumers and house purchasers owe could not have happened without some accompanying change in attitude towards it, can we say anything more about that change?

When is credit debt – or when is debt credit?

Credit may, then, be seen as moving from being viewed as dangerous to being morally neutral (a view which often carries the implication that those who can't 'handle' credit are themselves to blame), then to being 'beneficial' and thence to warranting a status and market of its own, independent of the goods for which the credit is intended.[17]

The evidence mentioned so far has mostly been drawn from the period since the election of the 1979 Conservative government, the period that has seen the largest expansion in the use of credit. However, the deregulation which that administration put in place, and its undoubted support for the expansion of the credit market, built on trends that were already well established, and which had indeed found their way into the accepted economic orthodoxy and statutory framework. For the Consumer Credit Act 1974 simply accepted the basically optimistic assessment of the Crowther Committee who reported that consumer credit made a 'useful contribution to the living standards and the economic and social well-being of the majority of the British people',[18] and ought therefore to be allowed to develop with the maximum freedom and the minimum regulation.

There have been contrary voices, not least ones basing their much more negative evaluation of the credit explosion on Christian, and specifically biblical, principles. In particular the Jubilee Centre in Cambridge has published a series of booklets which, while allowing some possibility for the legitimating of borrowing and lending, draw on the Centre's experience of dealing with families in debt to make proposals whose very titles

indicate that Centre staff see debt as something to be avoided,
rather than credit as an opportunity to be affirmed. To read their
book *Credit and Debt: sorting it out*[19] is to have an experience
very similar to that which people who suspect they may have a
drink problem have when reading about possible symptoms. The
Jubilee Centre has no hesitation in blaming the credit explosion
for the rise in the incidence of problem debt among poor families, and has made a series of recommendations to try and
counter it.[20]

In his account of the current research into consumer debt,
Graham Blount points out that negative attitudes to credit in
general are probably not widely held, although recent surveys
suggest an increasing number of people willing to say that 'credit
is too easy to obtain' (a view they might be very ready to discard
if they were personally refused it). Even the Jubilee Trust, in a
publication dramatically entitled *Escaping the Debt Trap: the
problem of consumer credit and debt in Britain today,*[21] while at one
level seeking to suggest that all credit is debt – 'It is highly
unlikely that credit cards would have become so popular if they
had been known as "debt cards" '[22] – nevertheless in an
unguarded note appear to accept the appropriateness of the credit
market when they say, 'Clearly not all debt is in any sense a
"problem". The major part of current borrowing is fully
expected to be covered by future income or asset sales.'[23] One
of the most important matters we shall have to consider is
whether debt that is 'not a problem' is in fact the ultimate source
of the debt that is; that is to say, even if not all credit is designated
debt, does not the increase in severe debt problems in society
have its root in the benign assumption that credit is beneficial
provided that it is 'fully expected' to be covered by future
income? We know, after all, what has happened to some of those
expectations and to the families and individuals who have had
to live with the consequences.

Indeed the ability to defend oneself against the suggestion that
one is in debt is widespread, even, and perhaps not least, among
those who are in danger of having a debt problem. In their work
on consumer debt, and in particular on student indebtedness,
Stephen Lea and his collaborators find ample evidence that the
impossibility (for all practical purposes) of avoiding debt while
being a student has generated a capacity, very similar to that in
the population at large, for being able to believe that certain

debts do not count as debts. A loan, such as the student loan, is not perceived as a debt – until, that is, you are a graduate faced with the need to start repaying it. Given the widespread assumption that in future all participation in the world of higher education will be by means of loans, students in general are unlikely to accept a designation of themselves as debtors with all the connotations of financial mismanagement. That students need far more education in 'realistic' budgeting and in the handling of their money is probably the only valid conclusion if there is to be no challenge to the fundamental assumption that credit is the right way for such expenditure to be financed. After all, as the National Westminster Bank affirmed in its slogan on the cover of the report of research into student debt – research which the Bank had supported – 'We're here to make life easier.'[24]

The weakness of financial education as a remedy for problems with debt, however, is that the evidence suggests that people are indeed being educated about debt, but that the education they are receiving comes principally from the constraints of their economic situation: they learn about debt by getting into it, and they get into it because they find they have to. This is a pattern of learning superimposed upon any other learning that students' time at university may offer them, and it is arguably the most influential learning they could be offered for the direction of the rest of their lives: they are learning to participate in the economy of credit and debt, and to accept it as a given. Davies and Lea find that the pattern of attitude change following the necessity imposed by students' financial circumstances leaves the researchers with a question, the implied answer to which is all too clear:

> Although [students] were not at first in favour of debt, to sustain an acceptable lifestyle, they found they had to go into debt. Once they had incurred debt, their attitudes to debt changed, so that they became more tolerant. It would be interesting to know what happens to these individuals when they leave university. Will they take a more tolerant attitude to debt with them . . . or will they take the opportunity to pay off student debts and, once free of debt, revert to a more typical anti-debt attitude?[25]

While their research specifically into student debt may leave them with this question, the examination of the general eco-

nomic psychology of consumer debt suggests that the answer
may not be far from what the less formal school of experience
would suggest. Lea, Webley and Walker find that there are indeed
differences of attitude to debt between those who incur serious
debt problems and those who do not, but it is not to these
differences in attitude that they find it most plausible to look for
a hypothesis about the *causes* of debt. That is not to say that
attitudes are completely irrelevant, only that they are nowhere
near as relevant as economic issues. For when they considered
the key economic variables within their research sample, they
found that

> debt is primarily found among people looking after families
> on low incomes in insecure housing. These conditions are
> associated with a set of behaviour patterns that make it
> harder to cope with them. Some people cope better than
> others, and the ways in which they do so may give us ideas
> of how people might be helped to keep out of debt. But
> for the most part, the psychology of debt forms part of the
> psychology of poverty, and any substantial reduction in
> the incidence of debt must come from a reduction in the
> impact of poverty.[26]

It may seem to reduce much careful research to a statement of
the obvious to paraphrase this conclusion in this way: you are
most likely to avoid debt if you have enough money. But given
the shame associated with not being able to manage your money,
and the accusations of irresponsibility often levelled against those
who find themselves in serious debt, that simple conclusion is
of the greatest importance.

Attempting to care – advice and education

> The 1991 [National Association of Citizens' Advice
> Bureaux debt] survey revealed that CABx were dealing with
> 100,120 problem debts per month. We are concerned at the
> evidence from CABx which shows that these debts are often
> most problematic for already vulnerable groups, noticeably
> disabled and elderly people, as well as those with low
> incomes. The harsh consequences of indebtedness are par-

ticularly severe when they come in the wake of social disadvantage. The CAB Service is concerned about the real inability for those on low incomes to make ends meet without resorting to credit use. We are, moreover, increasingly worried by the cost of that credit.[27]

The annual reports of NACAB reveal a steadily increasing demand for their advice and assistance, and show that in both absolute and relative terms problems with debt account for more and more of their work. Naturally the work is particularly labour-intensive, requiring, as well as attentive work with clients, negotiations with multiple creditors, public utilities, local authorities, finance companies, banks and building societies. Their evidence on debt and poverty, *The Cost of Living*, has all the authority of vast experience and measured presentation. But the stories which it includes are stories of desperation, of people crushed under a weight of debt, brought to the edge of suicide.

A CAB in Kent reports that a married man, a builder with three children, was facing the loss of his home, the failure of his business and possible bankruptcy. He missed his appointment with the CAB so the Manager phoned him as she knew there was further information he would need to have for his possession hearing. She was concerned by the tone of his voice and kept talking to him for quite a time. He agreed to come into the CAB to see her. When the Manager phoned, the client had been sitting by the phone considering suicide, with a shotgun in his lap.[28]

Such an example can be dismissed as extreme or deliberately dramatic. But its extreme quality does not make it distant from the experience of vast numbers of people in our society for whom unmanageable debt is indeed the extremity of desperation. The secrecy with which we guard our financial affairs has a great deal to do with the huge social stigma attached to not being able to sort out one's finances; beyond all others being in debt is an admission that it would be hard to make. But if this situation is hard for those who have been brought up to 'pay their way' and avoid debt, and yet find themselves trapped in it, we should not overlook that other group of people whose poverty is such that it never occurs to them that they could do *without* being in debt, whose lives are spent in a constant process of 'robbing Peter to pay Paul' as they juggle with a succession of bills and demands.

Theirs is an experience far removed from the mathematical formulae of annual percentage rates. Even adding up the total of their indebtedness is something to be avoided, partly because it is too frightening and partly because it is in any case irrelevant: the issue is to get to the end of the week, the next benefit payment, past the next collector. The CAB report *The Cost of Living*, and it is one of many such documents, is full of accounts drawn from the experience of clients who may not have reached the point of suicide but who are in fact in a trap from which they cannot possibly escape. Theirs may not always be the shame that goes with sudden indebtedness incurred by those who had thought to avoid it; but it is a constant life of impossible choices: are rent arrears a higher priority than the gas bill? Is paying the catalogue agent for the children's clothes now so urgent that it is best to risk not having money to pay for the electricity? What is to happen to a mother who is refused a loan from the social fund to buy a cooker on the grounds that she is (maybe rightly) not deemed able to pay the money back? Is she to go to a 'loan shark' and pay the enormous interest which that will involve? How is a family supposed to rent a home if a deposit is required, an item not eligible for a social fund loan, or rent in advance, for which loans are often refused?

And if a social fund loan is obtained and regular deductions made to recover it, what is likely to be the result given that benefit rates are in any case such as to leave very little room if any above the normal requirements for living? The statistics of the misery of those for whom debt is the inescapable context of life are a relentless sign of a society which assumes that provided a person can be lent money, that solves the problem. The result of this approach, revealed by debt survey, is that of those surveyed around two-thirds of unemployed people and disabled people, and more than four-fifths of carers, are in severe debt (meaning three or more debts).[29] The state of affairs which this situation brings about may not have the sudden extremity of the earlier near-suicide example, but the cumulative effect of indebtedness is just as desperate. Whether it is a couple with loan repayments amounting to £592 per month and a total income of £630 per month, and the man finally trying to take his own life, or the sole trader whose business has failed with nearly £63,000 of debts, his home repossessed and the relationship with his partner at an end, what we see is people who have been enabled and encouraged to see borrowing as the way of coping with their poverty, and who have then found that it simply makes their situation worse.

Out of such stories and such experience have come initiatives to try to ameliorate the situation. *The Cost of Living* is full of recommendations for legislation, for the amelioration of some of the worst symptoms of poverty, for controls on the activities of debt collectors and the disconnection policies of public utilities, for more imaginative means of assisting those with multiple debt problems to resolve their difficulties, for the mitigation of enforcement procedures so as to take account of the desperation of many multiple debt situations, and in general for the recognition by society that serious debt is with us and needs to be taken account of in social policy.

Behind such recommendations lie, as I have already said, the many hours of debt counselling and negotiations with creditors that assist individuals and those close to them to cope better in the situations in which they find themselves. In the process the counselling leads to an educational process in which clients acquire more personal strength, and distance from their current troubles, so that they are better able to resist those courses of action, such as resort to loan sharks, which could only make life worse. Nor are the CABx the only agencies which seek to offer personal assistance of this kind, and could therefore include their own stories of people and their desperation: organisations such as 'Credit Action', rightly acknowledging the wealth of biblical material that relates to debt and the management of money, also offer literature and advice to those who are, as they put it, in 'devastating financial bondage'.

Such work, on whatever basis, is absolutely crucial and further support of money advice agencies is essential if more and more individuals are not to become the casualties of the credit explosion. For what drives people into the kind of serious debt of which I have spoken, as all the research shows, is not an irresponsible tendency to over-commitment, but the lethal combination of desperate poverty and a society in which credit and debt – that is, the possibility of having what you need today on the basis of the assurance of tomorrow's, or next year's, income – are regarded as the appropriate way for society to grow and prosper. Yet advising individuals in trouble, and then making recommendations for ameliorating the situation of those experiencing problem debt, is too easily seen as the solution, at least by those at some distance from the process of advising clients; that is natural enough, for it does not address the complicity of those who on the face of it are managing the money very well and successfully. Those who offer help and education to individuals in trouble should not be criticised for offering all that can be offered, within the economy of which we are all part.

Attempting to care – creating an alternative

There are also those, however, who seek a way for community groups to enable borrowing and lending by those who do not have access to conventional sources of credit. Often motivated by their experience of debt problems in the communities where they live, they seek to create a means whereby people can save regularly and then borrow when they need to. They are bound by a legal requirement that credit unions are based on a 'common bond', that is a shared locality, or place of work, or interest. In exchange for regular monthly savings, members are able to obtain loans from the resulting common fund, at a rate of interest that cannot exceed 1 per cent per month on the reducing balance, a rate far lower than would ordinarily be available to the poorest members of the community.[30] It is clear that the credit union has never caught on in Britain to the same extent as in other countries. In the Irish Republic, for instance, at the end of the 1980s about 30 per cent of the adult population were members of credit unions; and significantly although the proportion is much lower in Northern Ireland it is about the same among Catholics there. By comparison the proportion in Great Britain is minute. By the end of 1987 only 108 credit unions existed in Great Britain, and in no region did the proportion of the population belonging to one approach 1 per cent.

As Berthoud and Hinton show in their research for the Policy Studies Institute,[31] there is a high level of idealism and commitment involved in and elicited by credit unions. There is naturally a running debate within the movement about whether credit unions are to be regarded principally as 'instrumental', the chief objective being simply the availability of opportunities to save and borrow, or 'idealistic', the chief objectives being to enable the poorest members of society to find a way out of their poverty and also to create a sense of community. These objectives are not of course mutually exclusive, and the evidence is that those who belong to credit unions value both aspects of their membership. They speak warmly of the sense of belonging which they gain, and those members who could save and borrow in more 'mainstream' ways, such as through banks and building societies, nevertheless regard the credit union as their preferred method of saving and borrowing.

On the other hand, there is a considerable cost involved, and the evidence for any belief that credit unions could offer a large-scale solution to problem indebtedness is not convincing. Most credit unions show the same tendency as other voluntary and community organisations to have the bulk of the work done by a small proportion of the members. It is also hard for the movement to be of assistance to those who are the very poorest, since in order to borrow it is necessary to have saved for a stipulated period, a requirement that is obviously going to exclude those who already have a great burden of indebtedness. It is therefore not surprising that the majority of members of credit unions are not people barred from other sources of credit, and for that majority, as Berthoud and Hinton show, there is not much financial advantage in doing their saving and borrowing through a credit union rather than through a bank or building society. 'For people denied access to mainstream credit, the comparison would be much more in the unions' favour. But most credit union members are not in that position.'[32]

I make this point in order to make a realistic assessment, not in order to decry the efforts of those who have enriched the lives of their communities by creating a degree of financial self-help. There are very good reasons for supporting alternatives to the banking system as a source of credit, and certainly to seeking ways round the worst excesses of money lending. The reality is that the credit and debt economy has taken such a hold on our society that making any substantial inroads into its territory will take time and commitment. I happen to believe that doing so is something of a gospel imperative, for reasons than I shall state later in this book, but for the foreseeable future it will always be possible for those who profit from the way things are to scoff at the slow progress of credit unions.

The mountain to move: the profitability of debt

For there is here also a cruel irony. Credit unions are, after all, a necessary attempt to reinvent a principle of mutuality, of lending out savers' money to borrowers within a community of borrowers and savers. This was, we should remember, what building societies were also supposed to be and what for a large part of their history they have been. They were (some still are) mutual organisations existing for the benefit of their members, lending to their borrowing members what their saving members invested. The Co-operative Movement and its bank, as well as the Trustee Savings Bank and the many mutual insurance companies and friendly societies, began with principles very similar to those now being encouraged, at great personal cost and on the basis of minimal resources, by the credit union movement.

At the same time as such efforts are being expended, we see the 'deregulation' of building societies and banks, and credit generally, being followed by the paying out of bonuses (in effect some of the reserves accumulated over generations of mutual ownership) as building societies and similar institutions are sold to new owners for whom the activity of lending and borrowing become not a community building activity but rather one of the most highly profitable of economic activities. For we are surely discovering that the disciplines of regulation were not arbitrary statutory rules imposed by an over-zealous government, but in effect the financial disciplines of living within your means, disciplines inherited from the past but now regarded as unnecessary limitations on growth. As we have seen in this brief examination of the vast explosion of credit and debt and its consequences, limitations on growth were also limitations on disaster. For the piggy bank, that derided symbol of the world we have left behind in the search for 'financial sophistication', imposed the very simple discipline that what was taken out could not exceed what was put in; applied to mutual organisations that discipline meant that there was a direct connection between what was borrowed and what was saved, expressed in the fact that those who carried out either activity, and in a lifetime people would expect to engage in both at different times, were alike 'members'. Of course such discipline meant that at times more wanted to borrow than could, and this is the phenomenon represented as 'mortgage queues' and 'rationing'; it is however the triumphant ending of that discipline that lies behind the vast extension of credit, and with it the vast expansion in the numbers of those whose lives are blighted by debt.

The world that has been unleashed around us is one in which the making of money out of money has become the most exciting world of adventure and the greatest source of wealth for the richest people in the world. Increasingly the balance shifts so that the activity of lending and borrowing – that is, the enabling of one person to use resources which at that time another does not require, but may require someday – is not what is carried on in order to support human beings in their personal lives and their productive activity, but is that for which life is engaged in. So it is not surprising to find that in the two decades to 1990, whereas income from wages has on average doubled, that from lending money has multiplied sevenfold.[33]

Because that is so, it is also not surprising that those with severe debt problems can be a source of profit to others who have encouraged them to take the most obvious and immediate, as well as illusory, ways out. Among those who resort to the accessible gambling of the National Lottery, with its hope held out of being free at one bound, will be those already in serious debt. The Saturday queues at Lottery ticket counters (presumably in fear of missing the one Saturday when they were going to be winners) are a witness not so much to simple greed for more money, but to a desperation to be free of a financial system that, having offered today what you will pay (more) for tomorrow, has in effect bound the future of all who are debt. The Lottery offers itself partly of course as fairy godmother, bestowing undreamt-of prizes on those who play, but also and more danger-ously as liberator of those whose tomorrow is already totally constrained by the enormity of what they owe today.

Other tempting ways out are the offers of further loans by institutions which exist to profit from the desperation of debt, and provide, in the process, a handsome return for their share-holders. Their solutions are less dramatic than the prospect of a

Lottery win, but are nonetheless powerful and profitable means of aiding the society of credit and debt. Consider this, for example, culled by a friend from the financial pages of *The Independent* in 1995, reporting the results of Provident Financial, which had increased its interim dividend by 69 per cent:

> Because Provident serves low income groups avoided by banks and building societies it is able to charge interest rates of more than 100%. Provident said demand was growing 'among lower income groups, which represent a growing proportion of the population'.[34]

These results were described by a leading analyst as 'super', and as a sign of the times they certainly are. I am not concerned here to set up an individual company for attack, or even to engender a sense of shame which this report so conspicuously lacks. This is not a report about loan sharks; many who make use of the services of 'the Provi' would be desperate without it. They see themselves as a family firm, and many families speak of having a good relationship with the firm and its collectors. But in its evident pride, untainted by any signs of guilt, that it is 'able' to charge such usurious rates it simply represents the logical extension of the idea that the market in money can be relied on to exercise the only necessary discipline over borrowing and lending. Maybe next year they will be 'able', with many others who seek to maximise the profitability of money, to charge 200 per cent interest. On the evidence, it seems likely that if they can they will.

This is the real source of our indebted society and all that flows from it: lending money has become the best way of making it, and there is a large constituency of people now with a strong interest in maintaining that situation. Meanwhile those who have enough money to manage have arranged their lives, their mortgages and their loans, so that to extricate themselves from basing today's consumption on tomorrow's income seems both impossible and unnecessary; and on the other hand those who do *not* have enough become more and more desperate as the weight of their poverty is increased by the size of their debt.

Conclusion: A faith to move a debt mountain

If it has been a heavy experience to read this account of the indebtedness that dominates our society, that will have been a reflection of the heaviness engendered in me in reading the stories of debt and how it works in people's lives, and then endeavouring to convey something of that in these pages. That weight, I suggest, extends wider than the bounds of our own national economy. As we shall see in subsequent chapters, it is to be felt globally as we contemplate what debt does to the inhabitants of the world's poorest countries, and what the pattern of thinking represented by credit and debt is doing both to the structure of human relationships and the connections human beings have with the natural universe of which we are a part. For the search for 'sophistication' and the abandonment of the derided piggy bank are without doubt precipitating us into a situation in which the disasters of the poorest, so far from being the result of their incompetence and failure, derive directly from the assumptions on which we base our lives and from the economic activity which reflects those assumptions.

That is to say, we are being precipitated into a crisis of faith, the point where the character of the assumptions on which we base our lives is being revealed, and where our main concern in this book, the revitalising for our time of the language of faith in Jesus Christ, meets the urgent need of our time for a basis, a set of life assumptions, a faith that will prevent the debt mountain and all it represents from defeating us all. For while hard-working and committed people seek to assist the most unfortunate victims of debt, whether through the compassion of their attention and advice or through the ingenuity of their attempts to establish mechanisms of saving and borrowing that enable people to be freer of indebtedness, the fact is that the forces committed to the relentless increase of the economy of credit and debt continue their efforts unabated.

This in turn underlines the second criterion which we gathered from Dietrich Bonhoeffer in our search for ways of speaking of Jesus Christ today: that however important it may be to offer solace and rescue to those whose lives have been reduced to weakness and distress, it is critical to continue the costly search for ways to speak with power and effect to those who represent humanity's strength in the marketplace. Unchallenged and

unchecked by the unconditional claim of Christ they will surely
defeat us all.

4

Loving and owing

As is apparent from Chapter 3, examining the distress which indebtedness inflicts on the lives of people and the high price credit exacts for enabling some to have today what they would otherwise have to wait for is a deeply discouraging experience. I have endeavoured to convey something of that discouragement in the last chapter, knowing that the depression induced by describing the pain which serious indebtedness inflicts still does not compare with the suffering of those for whom it is a daily personal reality; getting seriously into 'debt' as a research topic can only bring us within distant sight of what it is like to get seriously into debt as an experience. Nor is the credit and debt explosion in our own society all there is to describe. We shall have to turn in the next chapter to the global dimensions of this issue, where the distress, hidden and overt, is at least as dreadful to behold, and on a far vaster scale.

Yet before doing so it seemed important to return to some more general reflection on what we have seen, and in particular to begin the process with which this book is most fundamentally concerned: to seek the way in which Christ in his continuing life, and faith in Christ as a continuing reality, address this issue. For as we shall see in a later chapter, for all the difference there undoubtedly is between the economies of the biblical period and of our own, the reality of debt and its power to enslave were well perceived by our forebears in the faith, and the Bible and the early Christian centuries furnish us with much upon which to reflect in the process of liberating our economy from the power of debt. At this point, however, our purpose in reflecting on what we have seen and on some key themes in our Christian inheritance is to draw out a crucial contrast between what love, the name we give to our most basic experience of God, does for us and the very different entail of reliance on credit and debt.

The debt and credit that we experience are part of urban society as it has come to be. It is now the engine of economic development in industry, commerce and housing. Cities, indeed, are built on credit, and of course in Britain 'the City' – of London – is synonymous with the processes of making money out of money, its trading, its investment, and above all its lending and borrowing. Is it possible to ask the question, then, whether those economic realities are compatible with human loving and the experience of the divine love? Is it possible for there to be love in the city of debt?

Since love is one of Paul's 'three things that last' it should make no difference where it happens. If it can last through time, it ought also to be able to make its dwelling anywhere. Urban and rural loving should be much the same. In fact, many ideals of love seem to reflect a kind of suburban background in any case, the suburb being a kind of no-place and any-place.

Yet urban life is not generally felt to be very conducive to loving; the common life of urban dwellers, or, as Dan Hardy puts it, their *sociality*, seems to be rather more fallen than either created or redeemed.[1] Towns are lively, certainly, but not easy places for many aspects of human flourishing. They are places for exploiting, and for escaping from if people can afford it, where the sheer fact of having too many human beings in too close proximity to each other produces the same results as are found in overcrowded rat populations. For village dwellers a visit to the city can be a scary business, and the bigger the city the worse it is. Often people from Newcastle, for example, having visited London complain about the scale and the dirt and the noise, and are then surprised to learn that many rural Northumbrians make the same complaints when they pay visits to Newcastle.

Yet the visitors still come to cities, and even when they are at home in the country or the suburbs they nevertheless orientate their lives around things that can only be had because there *are* cities. Maybe too many people in one place at one time make for stress, for the transport and the drainage as well as other people; but how else shall we make our theatres and restaurants viable, how else deal with distributing the range of commodities and artefacts that have become the necessities of living and which mean that whether we like it or not we are all urban now?

And if love can exist anywhere, cities certainly cannot. They are built where rivers or railways made commerce possible, or where natural barriers made them defensible against prospective enemies and invaders. Love may seem to be the same wherever it happens, but again cities are not: they display in unavoidable starkness the economic character of their society and the social pressures under which it labours. Like the sun shining through a magnifying glass, they focus the strengths and achievements, the history and the prospects of nations; though like the sun shining through a window pane, they show up the dirt as well.

To ask whether there can be love in the city is therefore to try to bring together the timeless and the historical, the potentially ubiquitous and the inevitably local, so as to bring out all our strong ambivalence towards urban living. We cannot live without cities; that applies just as much to those who could not themselves bear to live in them. Yet how to sustain urban life in a loving and humane manner seems always to elude us. We perceive a conflict between the values of the gospel, which we seek to express in every time and every place, and the demands of historical conditions and the pressures of the locality. In that conflict it generally seems that the timeless is almost bound to lose. The demand for 'realism' (a term which only begs the question of what reality commands our first loyalty) excludes anything but a passing nod in the direction of 'vision'; though realism without vision is bound to lead to desperation or complacency.

Somewhere here there seems to lurk an error, a conception of love that confines it to the realm of religion or romance, and denies it the possibility of any real appearance within the world of time. Such a concept of Christ would once have been called *docetic*, a Christ only apparently human, and those who spoke in that way would have been called heretics. To expect to see love within the operation of the market or the campaigns of politicians and within the power structures and arguments that are demanded for the regulation of the city's life is actually to expect incarnation, of course, and that has always been a difficult conviction to hold on to.

So to ask whether there can be love in our urban life seems to require that we build time into love, so that time becomes not something love has to take into itself, but that which love itself contains and presupposes. Then, and only then, does it become possible to speak of love in the city without seeming to be joining together two essentially incompatible ideas, the eternal character of God with the historical character of social living. If love is itself temporal, however, then the Christ begotten before

the foundation of the world represents the constant orientation
of the creating and redeeming love of God towards the historical
flux and constant ambiguity that characterise the social inter-
course of human beings. In this chapter, a valley of reflection
between two mountains of debt, the domestic and the global, I
am concerned therefore to speak about love as something intrin-
sically temporal. It will then be possible to put alongside it,
comparing their effects, that ever larger mountain of debt which
we seem to need in order to build and sustain our cities, but
which also overshadows them. For credit and debt too, as we have
seen, are also essentially about retiming our resources, paying
tomorrow for what we can have today, or – for many – finding
ourselves unable to pay today for what we urgently need and
having therefore to commit tomorrow's resources in order to
survive.

Love's history

It is of the character of love to transport lovers out of history
into ecstasy, and it is of the character of our history that it
threatens our love with the invasion of disturbance and cares.
The capacity for ecstasy is dimmed, even destroyed, by the
damage of the past, the pain of the present and the fear of
the future, and all loving is thus vulnerable to the passing of time
and all that time brings. Yet the ecstasy itself engenders the hope
that love will last through the passing of the years, and participate
in the quality of endurance which is recognised as the key alike
to the loyalty of friendship and the faithfulness of a marriage
covenant; both thrust lovers into shared history, that for which
in their ecstasy they long. Yet the history which the lovers long
to share needs to be experienced as the fulfilment of their ecstasy,
not its enemy.

Rightly, Anders Nygren in his classic *Agape and Eros* resists
the tradition that makes *Agape* a merely moral quality, cut off
from its roots in the relationship of God with the world[2] 'Paul
is assuredly not a theologian of the Enlightenment, for whom
religion "is revealed as plain unvarnished morality"', he remarks
in opposition to Harnack's exposition of Paul's 'Hymn to
Agape' in I Corinthians 13.[3] On the other hand *agape* does not

become the love that lasts by being love for God rather than neighbour.

> Whether human love is one of the things that pass away, or one of those that abide, depends not on whether it is love for one's neighbour or love for God, but on whether it is a merely human love or a love born of God's own and in its image. If it is the latter, then it belongs to the things that abide, no matter what its object may be. It is not of this kind or that kind of Agape, but of Agape as such, of all Agape whatsoever as proceeding from God, that Paul says, 'Agape never faileth.'[4]

Love is therefore to reflect the divine love which is its origin, and that is to apply to love of neighbour as well as love of God. What is seen in that reflection is the quality of endurance and commitment which is not and will not be dependent on the changes of circumstances that inevitably accompany the lives of people and communities. Love is to survive, transcend and transform the occasions of failure and even betrayal which are the observed features of human relationships; that survival, through repeated acts of forgiveness, secures not merely the continuance of the relationship as though by cancelling a debt, but its enhancement by bringing new creation to pass when disaster threatens. In that way love repeats the dynamic of God's relationship with the elect people.

Love's most significant effect, therefore, is to provide an environment of security in which the unknown future of society can be faced. Life together requires a security in relation to that future, since what is quite certain is that the history which lies ahead will contain the same occasions of possible disaster as the past. The character of love is such as to enable the future to be entered into even in the expectation that love's demands will not be met, and that the high hopes to which love gives rise will be radically disappointed.[5]

This is the aspect of love which comes through most clearly in the most famous discourse on the character of love in the New Testament, presented by St Paul in his correspondence with the Corinthian Church. It is true, as David Ford writes, that

> . . . here precisely where he [Paul] is describing a 'still more excellent way' than service through various gifts of the

Spirit in the Church he resonates most deeply with the best in the general wisdom of his culture. Far from cutting the vision of 'common sociality' off from the specifically Christian, Paul sets a standard for the Church by it.[6]

Yet the characteristics of love, and particularly the way in which they contrast with those of other gifts of the Spirit, turn out to be ones which build on a specifically divine history. In that sense they have something to offer to society both then and now. What love offers according to this picture is space for the unknown future.

> Love does not come to an end. But if there are gifts of prophecy, the time will come when they must fail; or the gift of languages, it will not continue for ever; and knowledge – for this too, the time will come when it must fail. For our knowledge is imperfect and our prophesying is imperfect; but once perfection is come, all imperfect things will disappear.
>
> (1 Corinthians 13:8–10, NRSV)

Seen in the light of love's openness to the future, the words Paul uses in his 'Hymn to Agape', though they parallel descriptions of love offered by many of his contemporaries, take on a quite new significance.

> Love is always patient and kind; it is never jealous; love is never boastful or conceited; it is never rude or selfish; it does not take offence, and is not resentful. Love takes no pleasure in other people's sins but delights in the truth; it is always ready to excuse, to trust, to hope, and to endure whatever comes.
>
> (1 Corinthians 13:4–7)

What love does not do is focus on one's own achievements in the past (*boastful, conceited*), or the past failings of others (*pleasure in other people's sins*); it is not defensive of one's own present position (*rude, selfish, take offence, resentful*); it does not identify or fix one's own future by reference to what others already have (*jealous*). By contrast, what love does do is make space for the unknowable possibilities which the future holds for those who know the history of love as revealed in the dealings God has had with God's people (*patient, kind, ready to excuse, to trust, to hope, and to endure whatever comes*).

We are to be towards one another as those who do not know our own or each other's future, except that it is in the hands of the One who has proved trustworthy in the past.

When I was a child, I used to talk like a child, and think like a child, and argue like a child, but now I am a man, all childish ways are put behind me. Now we are seeing a dim reflection in a mirror; but then we shall be seeing face to face. The knowledge that I have now is imperfect; but then I shall know as fully as I am known.

(1 Corinthians 13:11,12)

So as God has revealed it, and in contrast with the gifts which were so greatly esteemed in Paul's Corinthian audience, love has a history, can face any history and will endure through all history. It is the way God keeps human history open.

In Paul's mind, this perception has enormous implications for the character of the Christian community; it is a community which can only be understood and whose essential character can only be lived out on the basis of a clear eschatology. Rightly, David Ford points to this severe lack in the Church of England's engagement with urban issues, as epitomised in the theology which undergirds its most significant and effective report on this subject in recent decades, *Faith in the City*.[7] For all its value in showing up clearly the grievous injustices faced by those living in Urban Priority Areas and expressing the Church of England's commitment to the inner city, the report is constrained by the ball and chain of the perpetual difficulty an established church has in taking seriously the eschatological dimension of faith.[8] Ford suggests that while it may be adequate to ground an address to the nation in the general moral requirements of justice and compassion, the report's address to the churches would have needed a far more explicit eschatology and a clearer statement of the Church's character.

Yet even to address the society in which we live on the subject of what it would mean for our cities, and our whole urban society, to be places of love requires an attention to the way in which Paul roots the concept of love in the history of God's people. If the gospel is not only for the Church but also for the world, the common cultural understanding of love requires the clarity of a specifically Christian critique. If the possibility of life together in a wholesome and sustainable setting depends on the city's foundation being love, then Dan Hardy is right to say, to society as well as to the Church,

> It is of great importance, therefore, that the foundations of the possibility of society be intelligently grasped, and the possibility thus revealed acted upon. Only thus may the direction of society be identified and pathological deviations discovered and remedied. To address this task is to ask about the position of society in the Doctrines of Creation and Redemption from which the issue of society has come to be disconnected.[9]

If, having looked at the character of love, we now look again at the nature of indebtedness as it has come to dominate our cities, we shall not be surprised to find there some of the strongest evidence of that disconnection and its resultant pathological deviations.

Debt: the binding of the future

Among the economic statistics eagerly awaited each month is the level of consumer debt. A significant increase in consumer debt is regarded as a sign that the economy is reviving, and is greeted with appropriate exultation by those responsible for the direction of economic policy. This is in some ways odd at a time when in other areas Victorian values are in vogue: evidently thrift and prudence are not necessarily high on the list. Yet the reason for this very positive attitude to consumer debt is that it is regarded as a reasonable index of public confidence: people will only borrow more, so the argument runs, if they are more confident in the future, if they expect their jobs to be secure and the property market buoyant. This very positive view of debt does not extend to public debt, government borrowing, which is regarded as a very negative phenomenon. It applies only to private debt, the debts of individual consumers. (It is worth noting in passing that the use of 'public' and 'private' in relation to debt is a particularly flagrant example of the individualism that accompanies a failure to identify the 'direction of society' and remedy its 'pathological deviations'; after all, how many individuals' debts does it take, and how large do they need to be, before they cease to be 'private' and become a matter of serious, 'public' concern?)

Many of those whose desperation I described in Chapter 3 would be astonished, first of all, to hear their indebtedness described as voluntary 'consumer debt' at all. For them, the view that their debt is part of a sign of renewed confidence in the future is (in the derogatory sense of the word) a myth. Persons in receipt of benefit do not borrow from the social fund, let alone from extortionate moneylenders, out of a sense of renewed confidence in the future but because of desperate need in the present. (In this respect, the debts of the poorest members of society resemble the indebtedness of the countries of the Two-Thirds World, to whom we shall turn in the next chapter.) Furthermore, the escalating indebtedness of students does not betoken the sense they have of their steadily improving career prospects on graduation but the necessary price of higher education. Any talk of indebtedness as a sign of confidence masks the large areas of society in which it is simply a sign of desperation.

Yet a critical examination of indebtedness which confined itself to the effect of debt only on the poorest sections of the community would be too limited. For surely as important as these personal effects of indebtedness are their wider consequences. A rising level of personal indebtedness in effect mortgages the future of the whole of society: as we have seen, it is itself the creator of social needs and the producer of great shifts in social attitudes. On the one hand, all of us who contract debts for whatever purpose limit our future freedom of action: if we have considerable debts to pay off, the pattern of our future life becomes largely determined. On the other hand, since we borrow against the hope of a rising standard of living and against the expectation of a steady increase in the price of property, those expectations *must* be met and those results *have* to be produced. As a result it is likely that whatever a government does in pursuit of those goals will be willingly accepted, whatever may be the accompanying costs in civil liberty or social justice. That is why I have made the point that among the many effects of lending money to the poorest and making students depend on loans for their education a predominant one will be social control: what chance is there of students being in the vanguard of social criticism if they all have huge debts to pay off?

I am not here, or indeed in this book as a whole, seeking to mount a doctrinaire attack on all forms of borrowing and lending, but to draw attention to the fundamental dynamic involved when the ideology of debt and the amount of it pass without examination. That dynamic is revealed in the original transaction by which those without food entered slavery:

> When that year was over, they came to Joseph the next year, and said to him, 'We cannot hide it from my lord: the truth is, our money has run out and the livestock is in my lord's possession. There is nothing left for my lord except our bodies and our land. Have we to perish before your eyes, we and our land? Buy us and our land in exchange for bread; we with our land will be Pharaoh's serfs. But give us something to sow, that we may keep our lives and not die and the land may not become desolate.'
>
> (Genesis 47:18,19)

The slavery which is the background to the Exodus and thus to the history of redemption results not from invasion or colonisation, but from debt. We shall see later that, whether as a result of that folk memory or because of other experiences, the Bible enjoins stringent controls on debt, on rates of interest, on the lengths to which creditors might go in seeking repayment, and on the length of time during which a debt could remain in force. Behind this is certainly the recognition of the dynamic of power that is involved in involuntary indebtedness, and more seriously still the effect that it has on the future freedom of action of the debtor. All the efforts of the ancient equivalent of social policy were directed at ensuring that debt was not a means to exploitation or to depriving others of their freedom for the future.

Thus the presentation of Christ as *redeemer* was not simply created out of the imagination, but was drawn from the deepest memories and contemporary experience of a people who knew what debt could accomplish and saw it as the reverse of the freedom which new life in Christ was intended to be. Lending and borrowing can, when the transaction is undertaken by two voluntary and equal participants, facilitate the best use of available resources; but it can only do that if its highly dangerous capacity to bind the future and impose the will of the creditor on the debtor are recognised and controlled. The point has a particular importance in a situation where most who enter credit transactions do so in the fond belief that they are doing so voluntarily: the pressures of an economy based on acquisition are such that the avoidance of debt is almost impossible, and the constraints of indebtedness on the future freedom of the debtor are so grave as to be something we hardly dare notice.

Ahead of us in the pursuit of the sociality symbolised by escalating debt is a society composed of two more or less clearly defined sections: on the one hand there are those with so much to lose and to protect that their capacity to see their own future as an open sphere of freedom is severely diminished; and on the other hand are those whose indebtedness has been forced to a level far beyond anything they might be expected to repay: they will be those with nothing to lose, whose future is simply a continuation of the bondage they already experience, and whose investment in society's good and society's laws will become minimal. Such is the effect of unrestrained debt on the very possibility of maintaining the fabric of anything called society.

Love and the freedom of the future

The nature of debt comes to the surface very quickly in any game of *Monopoly*. The possibility of buying and selling in fantasy the names of famous city streets is one that some, those with wealth, can find exhilarating; it is not so easy for those without wealth to have that sense of power – rows of upturned property cards marked 'mortgaged' are hardly ever the sign of a player with confidence in the future or much chance of surviving. (Similar games are available which reveal the way in which world trade works.) *Monopoly* surely survives because it is easier to relish the fantasy of large winnings than to savour the bitter fruits of bankruptcy.

In fact when the game was published in 1904 by Elizabeth Magie Phillips of Clarendon, Virginia (under its original name of *The Landlord's Game*), the phase with which we are familiar, that of rampant capitalism and acquisitiveness, was succeeded by a second phase in which, in accordance with the economics of

Henry George and the land tax proposals of Lloyd George's government, the site rents passed to the public treasury; this enabled a tax and benefit structure to be put in place under which, as the rules so touchingly say, 'Poverty and Unemployment disappear for ever.' Needless to say, this next phase of the game has not proved so enduring as the more familiar first phase – and the poverty and unemployment are still around too.[10]

Such a game is of course a caricature (though not as much of one as its inventor intended), bringing into high relief the reverse of that 'social transcendental' of which Hardy speaks. Any attempt to propose that a city might be built upon some other foundation, some form of social relation other than that between debtor and creditor, will immediately be branded either as sheer idealism or as the attempt to re-establish some form of repressive socialism presumed long dead. Such objections reveal the degree to which the economy now prevailing over our urban life rules in our minds and commands what amounts to worship. That economy and its rules together constitute a social transcendental other than God – an object of worship made by human beings, an idol chosen instead of the possibility represented by the Christian picture of love.

> We have already noticed how close is the relationship between ancient cities and idols – gods made by men – because they bear the same names. It is precisely by this creation of idols that the city closes herself up to God. Now she has her own God – the gods she has manufactured, which she can hold in her hands, which she worships because she is master over them, because they are the surest weapon against any other spiritual intervention.[11]

What Paul teaches, and what God has offered in Christ, is indeed a social transcendental which is in direct contrast to what such idols offer. It is a love which opens history up towards the future instead of locking the future up in an unequal distribution of power and resources by the fantasy of unlimited possibilities of affluence. For if that is the future in which the city chooses to lock itself it has indeed defended itself well against any possibility of 'spiritual intervention'. Such a 'society' is defended against all change except the unlikely one of revolution or the already evident signs of internal disintegration wrought by crime and social disorder. The links between acquisitiveness and crime, especially in the ambitions of young men, are well displayed by the example of Beatrix Campbell's account of 'joyriding':

> Joyriders' communication systems were built around the community on the one hand and technology on the other . . . Radio scanners gave the joyriders greater knowledge of police manoeuvres than the police could reciprocate.[12]

And she makes the point that only a fundamental consideration of the *meaning* of car crime and the way in which it connects crime and personal wealth will have any effect:

> In the absence of any challenge to the connections between the car cult, the potency of its pleasures, and their very identity as men, the criminal justice system was unlikely to impinge on these young offenders.[13]

The attempt to speak of love in the face of such realities runs the severe risk of sounding like a retreat into romanticism. The fear engendered in many parts of our urban environment, the places where nobody dares go, is such that it is hardly surprising that love is separated in our minds from anything that might be expected to be known in society, and the effects of those ideologies which have attempted to achieve sociality by planning and then imposing their plans is hardly encouraging. As Hardy writes,

> Given the ideologies and events of modern times, one might readily doubt whether there could be a transcendental sociality in the real which was either Godly or fully human.[14]

Yet it is in the face of that fact of our modern world view that Paul writes to the Corinthians of a way of being together that opens up the possibility of a new history. He speaks of a sociality that has to be real, to be practical; it starts, in the mind of Paul, with the Church as the community brought into being on the basis of the love revealed in Jesus, one that redeems those who were enslaved and whose future was constrained as a result of their indebtedness to false socialities. Paul's vision is of the Church as a society in which we shall 'owe no one anything but to love one another' (Romans 13:8).

If the social transcendental called love is to begin with the Church, it cannot end there; and the social project called Church has to be based on ideas and processes which might have the capacity to undermine that alternative sociality operative in society at large; the Church is to 'enable a dynamic growth to mutual love and hope.'[15] In constructing our life as Church we have to take account of the pressure upon the Church's members to conform to the life of the world and participate in its social reality. One of the realities which we may assume, therefore, is that our congregations will be composed of people who know something about love – and who also know a lot about debt.

So a start would be to talk about that reality openly and to begin to see how any possibility of being responsive to the call of God's future has been constrained for us all by the ways in which we have placed in bond the future Christ offers. And even as we try to face up to those realities, we shall also need to carry out another part of making the social transcendental a practical reality. What is fundamentally at stake is the rehabilitation and control of the economy of debt: to bring it within the bounds of mutuality, equality and concern for its effects. For what is involved is not just the alleviation of the dire poverty which the vast expansion of credit and debt occasions, but our answer to the question of who Jesus Christ is for us today in terms which will arrest and challenge the sources of economic strength as much as it supports and encourages society's economic victims. For however the concrete issues of credit and debt were handled in Israel and within the early Church – and to that we shall return – clearly those who experienced the social reality Christ brought into being discovered this reality to be such that people who had previously been burdened by debts they could never meet instead found themselves to be the recipients of treasure beyond price. There were others too who observed that new society, and *they* decided such a world would be too hard to control.

5

A world in debt

Throughout most of Africa and much of Latin America, average incomes have fallen by 10 per cent in the 1980's. The average weight-for-age of young children, a vital indicator of normal growth, is falling in many of the countries for which figures are available. In the 37 poorest nations, spending per head on health has been reduced by 50 per cent, and on education by 25 per cent over the last few years. And in almost half of the 103 developing countries from which recent information is available, the proportion of 6–11-year-olds enrolled in primary education is now falling.

In other words, it is children who are bearing the heaviest burden of debt and recession in the 1980's. And in tragic summary, it can be estimated that at least half a million young people have died in the last 12 months as a result of the slowing down or the reversal of progress in the developing world.[1]

As we have seen, to examine the escalation of debt in our own society can produce in us a sense of profound depression as we experience, even at a distance, the debilitating effect of rising levels of indebtedness on the lives of those who are its victims. When we come to examine debt in a global context we are confronted not just by debt the debilitator of people's lives, but by debt as a serial and multiple killer. It proceeds by undermining the best intentions of those committed to aiding the poorest nations of the world in the struggle to increase their standard of living, to provide for the most elementary needs of their population to be housed, educated and fed and to defeat the ravages of disease. It accentuates the economic and class divisions of the poorest societies, and pits the poorest of the world against one another in a struggle for what remains of the world's resources after the insatiable appetite of the world's debt economy has devoured their much-needed sustenance. But as we shall see yet again, it is not sufficient to pay attention to the plight of the victims of global indebtedness, desperate as that often is; it is the world's creditors, not just its debtors, who need to be considered.

Oil and interest: the fuels of the debt explosion

> As a loan officer, you are principally in the business of making loans. It is not your job to worry about large and unwieldy abstractions, such as whether what you're doing is threatening the stability of the world economy. In that sense, a young banker is like a soldier on the front lines: he is obedient, aggressive and amoral.[2]

Thus a young American banker looks back on what it was like in the business of international loans, 'selling money door to door at the edge of the civilised world'. Lucrative for him and for his bosses, the trade in money and its rapid expansion during the 1970s is often named as the root of the current crisis. If that is not seen, the remedies likely to be proposed will surely be wide of the mark, and will focus in inappropriate ways on the contribution allegedly made by victims or on the unavoidable consequences of 'acts of God' – inhospitable climates, earthquakes and other natural disasters. Considered in that way, the debt problems of the countries of the Two-Thirds World may indeed elicit pity and even generosity on the part of those who encounter them; but in effect our response will be fatalistic, and we shall speak of the indebted much as we have misused a biblical text in order to say (with resignation as much as regret) that we shall always have the poor with us. The regret and resignation may well be genuine, but they will also be self-serving, focused on offering remedies for human weakness in the face of an uncontrollable world and leaving on one side the responsibility of articulating the claim of truth upon the way of life chosen by the strong.

Of course there is a contribution that has been made to the problem by the governments of debtor countries. It would indeed be foolish to deny the role of corrupt élites and oppressive regimes in aggravating the crisis of international debt. Their love of prestige projects, whatever the relevance or irrelevance of these projects to the actual needs of their people, their resort to high levels of military expenditure not least in order to ensure their own survival, and their practice of financial self-aggrandisement, have all been part of what has saddled their countries with burdens of repayment which they have no prospect of being able to bear.

Equally, however, we have to ask what the governments of what are now the debtor countries could possibly have been expected to do in the circumstances with which they were faced in the 1970s and since. The sudden rise in oil prices at the start of that decade left the bankers of the oil-rich countries with enormous sums of money (the 'petro-dollars') for which to seek a use, and with low interest rates prevailing at the time and eager sellers of money travelling the world in search of borrowers it looked like an offer nobody in their right mind would refuse. Here was a chance to carry out the advice of nearly every expert whom impoverished countries consulted about their development needs: to industrialise, to develop an advanced infrastructure, and to seek by means of large capital projects to cater for the present and future needs of their fast-expanding populations. At the rates of interest prevailing at the time, there seemed every prospect of managing the debt.

Yet to carry out this almost universal advice meant acquiring loans and thereby being in the power of those who made them. As we shall see, that power has now come to mean the need to submit their domestic economic policy to the external controls imposed by the creditor countries and by the international agencies they control, such as the World Bank and the International Monetary Fund. But even before that happened debtor nations were in the power of their creditors in the sense that they had no control over the interest rates which they had to pay. That fact tied the debtor nations directly into the economic policies being pursued in the most powerful creditor nations, notably the United States and Britain. Under these, in the context of the progressive deregulation of financial services, interest rates had become the main means by which to control inflation. As we have already seen, that particular instrument laid very heavy burdens on the backs of those who had borrowed money to buy houses and consumer goods; what it did also was to make what had seemed irresistibly tempting financial deals entered into in the 1970s turn into a nightmare, a nightmare that endured and worsened through the following decade and is still with us.

Part of that nightmare was the further oil price rise that took place at the end of the 1970s, giving a further twist to inflation. The only means of controlling inflation available to governments set on a course of financial deregulation is their control of interest rates, and these were manipulated whenever it was felt necessary for domestic purposes – often for domestic *political* purposes – without the slightest reference to the effect of interest rate movements on poor countries burdened with the debts they had been encouraged to take up. So whereas the period of low interest at the end of the 1970s, lower than the rate of inflation, meant that it paid to be a borrower, the lower inflation and higher interest of the 1980s meant that debtor nations were now stranded with very expensive loans: every time real interest rates (the difference between the nominal interest rate and the rate of inflation) increased by a tenth of one per cent, anything from $2 billions to $6 billions were added to the debtor nations' debt charges.[3] So even as nominal interest came down in the second half of the 1980s, the real interest rates continued to be crippling, and meant that new loans had to be negotiated, in much less favourable conditions, to pay off the old ones. Susan George makes the point that even those countries with oil reserves which were then much more valuable, such as Mexico, Venezuela or Nigeria, paradoxically became more indebted as they borrowed more money to develop their oil industries and thereby became in the eyes of the world banking system economies worth lending money to.

So the game of 'blame the debtors' evades the role of the economic history of the period, one in which even the most virtuous regimes of debtor countries would have had little choice but to take on the burden of debt they did. What is more, the corrupt and dictatorial regimes which used the money lent for purposes that had nothing to do with the well-being of their people, such as prestigious projects and military hardware, may be obvious targets for blame; but in such cases we need to ask too about the complicity of the lending countries in the maintenance of such governments in power. For it is a fact that it is often in the interests of the lending countries to maintain in place regimes which may be out of touch with, or even hostile to, the needs of the poor, simply because they serve the geopolitical interests of the lending powers themselves.

In the international lending bids, metropolitan banks gave preference to authoritarian clients. These generals provided solid guarantees that nationalists and leftists would not get in the way of repayment. They also demonstrated that their military muscles could be used against their own people to squeeze them out for repayment. . . . Thus was formed a peculiar alliance of international bankers, military élites, military industrial bosses and local financial operators favoured by the generals.[4]

Yet after the blaming of the victim, creditor nations are apt to move to the second position in the search for causes: to say that debt is the result of the misfortune of the debtor countries in simply lacking the climatic, mineral, agricultural and other resources which they would have needed to avoid becoming trapped in the inability to repay. With the active support of their political and financial establishments, populations of creditor nations are likely to look out over the nations of Asia, Africa and Latin America and, having taken due note of all the incidents of genocide, civil war and military government, to see as further 'reasons' for the crises of debt and poverty the vivid pictures of earthquakes, floods and other natural disasters and to say to themselves that it is sad but cannot be helped.

But nature is not so one-sided a participant in this drama either, nor has it dispensed its gifts and disposed its catastrophes on its own. For many debtor countries are in fact rich in raw materials, and blessed with bountiful soil and mineral deposits. Yet one of the determining factors in how those resources are used is precisely the economic relationship which such countries have with the lending powers. For example, when debtor countries turn to the International Monetary Fund for assistance when the burden of repayments becomes too great, they are invariably required, in exchange for the assistance they need, to devalue their currency and thus reduce the price of their exports, not least their exports of raw materials.[5] Thus the creditor countries, while continuing to demand repayment of their debts, in fact gain the advantage of a situation in which raw materials are made cheaper and cheaper for them to purchase, while the debtor countries are led to competitive devaluations against each other. The World Bank is particularly committed to this kind of solution; Susan George and Fabrizio Sabelli, in their analysis of the policies of the Bank, cite the example of what happens when Kenya is induced to devalue its currency, thereby reducing the export price of tea, and when Sri Lanka is then required to do the same. The two debtor countries end up in competition with each other – while the creditors get the cheaper tea![6]

The notion that the debt crisis is somehow the *result* of a lack of natural resources available to the debtor nations is an illusion. The fact is that the debt crisis has been the *cause* of the progressive loss of value for the debtor countries and their peoples of the indigenous resources of their countries; while they have received less and less for the resources they sell to the creditor world, they also have to pay more and more for what they need to import from creditor nations. The reality is that the economic relations between creditor and debtor nations are such, and the processes of competitive devaluation so persistent, that the creditor nations have gained in cheap raw materials and primary products far more than they could ever expect to have had repaid.

> The debt has already been largely or entirely paid. The North is, in fact, substantially in debt to the South since it has received, since 1982, the cheapest raw materials on record and the equivalent of the value of six Marshall plans, net, from the indebted countries.[7]

At the beginning of this section, I described oil and interest as the *fuels* of the explosion of international debt. This is not the same as saying that the debt crisis *originated* with the oil price rises of the 1970s or with the interest rate fluctuations of the 1970s and 1980s. For the effects of those admittedly momentous events were determined not by the events themselves but by a set of assumptions about how the wealthy and powerful should relate to the world. M. P. Joseph, from whose 'Third World View' of the debt crisis I have already quoted, describes most forcefully the combination of attitudes which themselves determined how the events of those two decades would be handled. He points out that at the time, and to some extent still, the Banks were seen as performing the great service of recycling surplus money in such a way as to meet the development needs and offset the balance of payments deficits of the poorest nations.

But that way of presenting what happened simply conceals the truth.

> This is a carefully cultivated myth; or, a myth cultivated to isolate the debt trap from colonial domination, its new ideological equivalent known as development and the dependency relations. Colonialism, development ideology, dependency and debt crisis are structurally linked and operate as different shades of a single mechanism to promote the drainage of wealth from the poor to the rich.[8]

The important point about such linked attitudes and policies is that it is perfectly possible with the best possible intentions to participate in processes, in this case of lending for development, without noticing until too late either their self-serving nature or their disastrous consequences.

Global fallout

> In more readily comprehensible terms, this means that for an entire decade the 'developing' world debtors have remitted on average to the industrialised countries $12.2 billion a month, £3 billion a week, $406 million a day, $17 million an hour, $283,000 a minute.[9]

Thus Susan George endeavours to convey the continued worsening of the international debt crisis. In a sense she cannot write her books fast enough: these words are from the 1994 foreword to an updated edition of a book first published in 1988, and all she can report is that the trends she indicated then have continued and accelerated. She is well aware that there can be debates about the details of her figures: some would point out for example that her total of a trillion and a half dollars transferred in debt service payments from the debtor to the creditor nations includes not just interest but capital repayments as well. But all that does is to reduce the $283,000 a minute to a 'mere' $100,000 a minute. Statistically that is very significant, of course; but for those directly affected, who are

> losing their land, having to leave their villages, watching their children waste away, working fourteen-hour days for

next to nothing or not working at all, drinking polluted water, suffering from hunger and avoidable disease, being imprisoned or tortured or murdered if they speak out or try to change their lot,[10]

disputes about the precise statistics are simply diversions from the simple truth that the situation created by the international debt crisis is disastrous and becoming more so all the time. Hard though it is even at second and third hand, it is necessary that we record at least some of the range of human catastrophes that the debt crisis of which we have been speaking can engender. For it is very easy otherwise to assume that the human catastrophes, the famines and disease, which we see vividly pictured on our television screens, are simply instances of the problem of world poverty, and not directly related to the issue of international debt. Yet the testimony of those who watch and experience the suffering of the poor makes very clear how closely linked it is with the financial requirements imposed by indebtedness, and the fundamental injustice of these.

So for example the Archbishop of São Paulo, Cardinal Paulo Evaristo Arns, interviewed in 1985 for a Swiss newspaper, put the relationship very clearly:

The huge effort of the past two years resulted in an export surplus of a billion dollars a month. Yet this money served only to pay the *interest* on the debt. It's impossible to go on this way; we have already taken everything the people had to eat, even though two-thirds of them are already going hungry. When we borrowed, interest rates were 4 per cent; they're 8 per cent now and at one point they went as high as 21 per cent. Even worse, these loans were contracted by the military, mostly for military ends – $40 billion were swallowed by six nuclear plants, none of which is working today. The people are now expected to pay off these debts in low salaries and hunger. But we have already reimbursed the debt, once or twice over, considering the interest paid. We must stop giving the blood and the misery of our people to pay the First World.[11]

These words come from the experience of Brazil, and they put briefly all the issues which the international debt crisis has thrown up. The requirements imposed by creditor nations and banks, and then by the World Bank and the International Monetary Fund, mean turning the economies of poor nations towards export drives. As the Archbishop's words make clear, huge efforts expended in that direction can still only service the debt; they cannot repay the capital. Like the homeowner with an 'interest-only' mortgage, the future for poor nations can only be a continuation of the past; they have to go on paying interest, a burden from which they will never be free, in an amount over which they have no control – at the time the Archbishop was speaking interest rates were double what they were when the loan was taken out, and from time to time will, if the needs of the creditor economies require it, take off into the stratosphere. We see also in these words a statement about the complete irrelevance of the original loan to the needs of a population in poverty: military hardware and nuclear plants with all that they imply in danger and obsolescence mainly serve the needs of First World exporters. And the overall result is this: payments to creditors in interest charges that far exceed the amount of the principal loaned in the first place, achieved at direct cost to the people in hunger and deprivation.

This book began with a story from Kenya, with workers on pineapple plantations suffering serious damage to their health from the chemicals they were required to use so as to enable consumers in the First World to enjoy pineapples at any time of the year they wished. Those interviewed about their situation may not have had the ability of the Archbishop of São Paulo to connect their plight with the operation of the international economic system; to them it may simply have been the mysterious effect of a cocktail of chemicals which they were required to use with neither the knowledge nor the safety equipment to protect themselves from the consequences of their daily exposure to it. What was clear, however, was that their political leaders were well aware of the consequences of any public exposure of this issue for an export trade which was essential to Kenya's ability to pay its way – and that meant to service its debts – in the international economic arena.

The libraries of aid agencies groan with accounts of research, pamphlets, booklets, and letters from their partner agencies in Third World countries that describe essentially the same phenomenon. The money was there to lend and so it was lent. It was lent in ways that would benefit creditor countries with their own needs to export, to develop profitable international markets, and above all to find a safe and rewarding home for their money. The results vary from country to country, but the effect of debt is always the same: the diversion of resources away from the meeting of need.

This may not always lead to the kind of catastrophe that can be described in the terms used about Brazil; in a middle-income country such as Jamaica, while life expectancy may be generally good it is nevertheless the case that access to health care is very limited, to the point that churches and voluntary agencies are having to provide voluntary clinics. But how can it be sustainable for any country over a period to have to spend half of its government budget on debt servicing, as was the case in 1992, or even to find as it did in 1995 that it was spending four times as much on debt servicing as on health care?[12] Even if it is true that Jamaica is in the (relatively) fortunate position of being able to reduce its total debt burden over time, the effect of debt will have been to determine the priorities of government and people over a long period, with all that that implies for the loss of democratic control and responsibility.

It is precisely because it is not a country generally thought to be experiencing disaster that Jamaica can demonstrate the power of debt most clearly. Prior to the 1970s many problems in the Jamaican economy were being tackled, though unemployment remained a growing issue. But in the period following the oil price rises in the early 1970s, the external forces ranged against the Jamaican economy increased: because of the oil price rise the cost of imports trebled in the year 1973 to 1974; exporting became more difficult because of the worldwide recession, and interest payments increased. The crisis could most obviously be met by borrowing, and it was (not least because Jamaica was seen as a good credit risk), with a consequent increase in the costs of debt servicing and repayment.

The International Monetary Fund, approached for assistance, imposed its own standard prescription as a condition for the loans it was asked to approve. Imports were to be cut, exports increased, government spending drastically reduced to control inflation, even as price controls on commodities essential to the poor were relaxed. So social spending was cut, with the inevitable effect that the government fell, to be succeeded by a more right-wing one, committed to the IMF prescription. But this too was unable to meet the demands of that prescription at the pace the IMF imposed. So a population whose country is in debt through no fault or decision of its own inevitably loses the capacity to order its own affairs. The Finance Minister's description of the effect of the attempts to implement the IMF's progressively more stringent provisions for the structural adjustment of the economy could be repeated in country after country around the world, all of whom have faced 'the reordering of the priorities of the government away from long-run goals of growth and redistribution of income to short-run problems of the management of inflation, debt and the balance of payments'.[13] This comment will turn out to describe not simply what happens to have taken place in economies subject to disciplines imposed by indebtedness but the conviction of economists in creditor countries and international institutions about what is best for any economy anyway.

But the selection of a 'middle-income' country as an example to illustrate the almost universal effect of indebtedness on an economy must not blind us to the fact that ultimately such burdens issue in lethal violence. It is not hard to see that the need to service debts imposes huge burdens on social stability; Kenya, as already mentioned, does not find it convenient to have investigations going on into the safety record of international companies which contribute to its export income. The destabilising effect of that ends again and again in war. Ethiopia is the poorest country in Africa, indeed its gross national product is only about $110 per person; but in that context it is still possible for its government to find it necessary to spend $13 per person on waging war in Tigray and Eritrea, while less than half that amount is spent on health.[14] And military expenditure to control the social instability produced by debt simply produces, of course, as well as untold death and human suffering, yet more debt.

'You can't buck the market'

Quite rightly our eyes are drawn to the consequences of international debt by an awareness of and then a concern for the plight of the victim countries and peoples. We see pictures and read accounts of their deaths, of their loss of control over their own destiny as their nations fall into the hands of military regimes or as they are driven to elect governments who will find ways of complying with the demands of creditors, of their loss of civil liberties as their rulers feel driven (even if that is not their first instinct) to prevent any opposition to policies which will allow loans to be obtained and debts to be serviced, of their inability to make progress in meeting their people's needs for education, jobs, health and welfare. We read and hear about these things, and in some cases see them vividly depicted, and we know that these and many other results of chronic indebtedness are in and of themselves sufficient reason for the world to pay attention and to bend all its resources of ingenuity to alleviate the burden of debt borne by the poorest nations.

Yet time and again those who have campaigned for almost any measure of remedy for the debt trap are faced with what seems like an almost religious aversion to doing anything that might be effective. It is for this reason that George and Sabelli in writing about the activities of the World Bank make it clear that they are engaged not in a personal attack on the staff of that institution, or indeed of many others who believe that in providing loans for the poorest nations they are facilitating their development, but rather in a critique of an entrenched orthodoxy, as powerful and pervasive as were the orthodoxies of religious empires, an orthodoxy that is almost impervious to counter-evidence and to which all alternative convictions appear to be heresies.[15] It would indeed be an injustice to those involved to suggest that they were simply out for what they could get or determined to be as exploitative as possible of the world's most vulnerable. It is not in that sense *evil* that the indebted of the world are up against, but a form of sympathetic regard which, however, cannot sacrifice its commitment to a way of seeing the world that is simply inadequate to the crisis that faces us.

Set at the heart of this orthodoxy is the conviction that there is a world market which is generally beneficent in its effects and certainly unalterable. There is no alternative to it; or at any rate those alternatives that have been proposed hitherto – such as command economies of the left, or protectionist interference with free trade – all have consequences which are ultimately destructive. This is a particularly difficult belief to challenge, as whatever consequences follow from the working of the market can be represented as 'just the way things have fallen out'; as with the weather, you can complain about it or wish it were different, but you cannot alter it. And following from that almost religious conviction about the operation of the market there comes an equally powerful moral conviction that the right way to live is to follow the rules of the market.

Chief among those, of course, are the rules that debts are to be repaid, and contracts specifying the terms of repayment are to be honoured. So any proposal to lift the burden of debt has, as we shall see, to counter the charge that it is undermining two of the essential rules by which trade is regulated. That will mean, so the argument will always run, that lenders will be unwilling to enter into agreements to lend money; that investors will not be willing to invest in development; and ultimately that trade, which is believed to be the key to improving the quality of life of the world's poorest, will be destroyed. So, since there is no means of lifting the burden of indebtedness currently borne by the poorest nations which does not involve remission or cancellation of some debt, the argument runs that any such action will involve a breaking of the rules and therefore the setting of a precedent which will then be appealed to by every borrower who wishes to escape from a debt previously incurred. It is an international version of the argument advanced by water companies for their retaining the right to disconnect supplies for non-payment of water bills: 'If we do not have the power to disconnect, nobody will pay their bill.'

Yet there have to be very special features of a conviction or a moral rule that make it apply against all evidence and in spite of any consequences. And one special feature in this case, clearly, is that the evidence and the consequences do not appear to be affecting directly those who enforce the conviction and apply the rules. That is, the convictions are held, and the rules enforced, in an environment that seems far removed from the terrible deprivations which the debt trap imposes on the world's poorest. It is easier to believe in the free operation of the market, and the crucial importance of sustaining the obligations of contract and the duty of repayment, in a setting of relative prosperity; those saddled with the cruel burden of repaying debts that were neither incurred with their consent nor used for their benefit will see things from a different perspective.

Caveat creditor – the explosion comes home

The regime of credit and debt has effects on creditors as well as debtors. For the debtor economies have had to institute policies to make it possible for them to service their debts, and those policies are not always in the long-term interest of those whose commitment to the repayment of debts makes the policies necessary. The impoverishment of workers in the debtor economies, for example, makes it highly profitable for industries to transfer production out of the First World and into the Third World, whatever the conditions of service of employees. For example, if Mexico is to service its debt, which is about 75 per cent to US banks, it is hardly surprising that it will follow the policies recommended by the IMF, allow low wages and social benefits and thereby increase its exports. But there is a downside back home among the creditors. The transfer of employment between the United States and Mexico is but one of many such examples:

> Tens of thousands of American workers have lost their jobs and tens of thousands more have seen employment opportunities vanish, as US companies transferred production to Mexico to take advantage of the poverty of Mexican workers and the absence of any effective regulations on corporate behavior.[16]

So the continued downward pressure exerted on poor economies by the burden of debt will inevitably depress the standard of living of workers in industrialised economies who have to compete against the wages and working conditions of those who live in countries desperate for increased exports at almost any price. But this is far from the only 'Debt Boomerang' effect to which Susan George draws attention in her book of that title. We should not be surprised to find that the pressure for export revenue leads to environmental effects which amount to little short of the destruction of some of the most varied, interesting and productive ecosystems in the world. To take but two of George's examples, there is a direct connection between indebtedness and the rate of deforestation, such that in the 1980s Brazil, leading the ranks of international debtors, increased its rate of deforestation by 245 per cent, and large increases are to be found in several other debtor countries; the only ones in which the rate has not increased are those which have already lost most of

their forest anyway.[17] George also documents the extent to which
the debt-management policies of creditor countries, and their
agencies like the World Bank and the International Monetary
Fund, plan and execute, through dependent governments in
Third World countries, economic policies which end in the
destruction of species and natural resources. Although the patterns of consumption in wealthy countries are themselves
environmentally destructive, their effect is not as great as that
arising from the immense economic leverage produced by the
debt crisis.

Although individual lifestyles in the developed countries
can be held partly to blame for environmental destruction,
we believe that it is above all the actions of the Northern
creditor governments, and those of the international institutions they largely control, which drive the forces behind
this destruction. They invented the initial 'development'
model which has led to ecological disaster. They have used
the leverage provided by the debt crisis to perpetuate this
model.[18]

Probably the most sinister double message sent out by the
creditor countries' debt-management policies and the programmes they impose on the debtor countries is about the trade
in drugs. It is not necessary here to set out the vast increase in
drug abuse that pervades the countries of the north. Politicians
unite in condemning the drugs trade and in lending verbal
support to attempts by authorities in countries where the raw
materials of the trade are grown to suppress the trade. We are
used to extensive media coverage of the activities of 'drug barons'
and the crime spawned by drug dealing, not to mention the
violence that stalks our own cities as well as the cities of countries
in the grip of the drug trade. We are glad to hear of more and
more extensive international police co-operation in the fight
against the trade. We are beginning to grasp that of all criminal
activity that involving drugs is the most 'classless'; paying very
high school fees is no guarantee of reducing, and may indeed
increase, the chances that one's child will become involved in
the taking of drugs and even in trading them.

But even as we are aware of these things and support what
we believe to be remedial action against them, those who decide
the economic policies to be applied to the management of

international debt press on with programmes whose effect must be to make debtor countries more and more beholden to drugs traffic. In Bolivia, the poorest countries in Latin America, for instance, it is estimated by the government itself that in effect one job in every three or four is provided by the trade in coca, some half a million jobs; and to these must be added around half as many again arising indirectly from that economic activity, which itself earns more than the country's entire agricultural production. No wonder influential politicians in the country believe that the end of the drugs trade would mean unemployment and social unrest on a massive scale.

Yet this story is not simply to be read as the effect of poverty. The growing dependence on the coca trade is the inevitable result of the collapse in the market price of tin, Bolivia's previous main export, together with the structural adjustment imposed on it by the International Monetary Fund. The austerity, and the cuts in wages and public services which are the standard demand of the IMF in dealing with massively indebted economies, could only be sustained at all because the large drugs economy was generating substantial earnings. It must be one of the greatest ironies that a press statement could be issued by the IMF in December 1989 praising the Bolivian effort and saying this: 'Since the start of the economic reform program in late 1985, Bolivia has made substantial progress in *correcting financial imbalances and economic distortions*.'[19]

When it is a 'correction' to enable former tin workers to take to the growing of coca, we know that we are in the presence of creditor-speak. What had happened is that *petro-dollars*, loaned to a military regime, used principally for the purchase of military equipment and consumer durables from manufacturers in creditor countries, were being repaid in *narco-dollars* generated in the process of servicing the market of the very countries which claim to be doing all they can to bear down on the drugs trade. But this is not apparently so important as to outweigh the observation made a few sentences on in the survey of the satisfactory completion of what to the creditor countries and their agencies is the key task: 'The current account deficit of the balance of payments has narrowed over the period, and Bolivia has sharply reduced its external debt to commercial banks and certain bilateral creditors.' Similar stories can be told of the economies of other drug-producing countries, and of course this particular 'boomerang' is closely connected with the ecological one to which we have already referred: for if the drugs trade is going to be the most successful way of meeting the demands of a nation's creditors, it is bound to seem highly attractive to make over forest lands to growing coca.

And so continues the tale, and the entail, of debt; in an interconnecting spiral of relationships and developments a certain way of running the world, a set of convictions and rules, generates situations of great suffering for debtor countries and their populations, threatening them with starvation, social and political instability, the undermining of democratic sovereignty and the subordination of their social needs, education and health in particular, to the insatiable demands of their creditors. But at the same time these very same policies are sowing the seeds of social destruction in the very countries which are imposing the policies. Not only does the debt trap result in the loss of jobs and markets to those places where in the desperate struggle to increase exports wages are kept low, not only are debtor countries driven to engage in the cultivation of drugs to be sold in the streets and playgrounds of the creditor countries, but further contradictions and ironies surface as well.

Deals are done with banks[20] under which debts which are unlikely to be repaid are purchased at a discount by their governments. This trade in financial 'paper' does not of itself result in any remission of the debt to the debtor countries, and is for the most part carried out by the same governments that are at the very same time seeking to reduce public expenditure. It has all the marks of occasions when indebted individuals engage the charitable efforts of churches and trusts to bail them out; what in fact happens is that charitable money is used to insulate the lending institutions from the consequences of the risk they took in making the loan. On other occasions, they may well plead that risk as justification for the interest they charge to borrowers![21]

Not least among the global consequences of the deprivation imposed by the debt crisis are the unprecedented refugee and migrant populations of the world. Some of them we count as 'refugees' or 'asylum seekers', while others we do not. Among those we do count are those fleeing from wars which, as we have seen, too often owe their origins at least in part to the political instability and strife caused by the extreme measures debtor countries have to take in order to meet the requirements of their creditors. But others are deemed to be 'economic migrants', people for whom the world's refugee conventions allow no space. Their loss of home or possessions may indeed be due in part to the economic pressures on their own countries; what is certain is that the debt crisis produces an increasing level of poverty which in turn generates the unprecedented migrations that the end of this century is seeing. Naturally, that boomerangs onto the international community in the need they then feel to police ever more stringent immigration provisions, and in the pressure on them to send aid to those who are living in wretched camps having been driven from their homes.[22]

We are not invited, when we are addressed with appeals to our compassion for the world's refugees and displaced, to devote much attention to the question, 'Why?', and yet it is a critical one for us to address. Enormous energy is spent by the governments of creditor countries on processes designed to keep migrants, especially economic migrants, at bay. It is quite evident that these processes often lack humanity, and that they are becoming increasingly draconian as the ranks of humankind on the move grow before our very eyes. For the increasing efforts devoted to the control of migration, and the ever-increasing burdens borne by refugee agencies and by countries, often themselves very poor, which neighbour on areas of conflict or severe deprivation, are in large part the result of the way in which a world economy dominated by debt begins to damage the lives of all.

At the top of any list of the disastrous ways in which the debt trap eventually comes home we must however place the connection between debt and war. For while it is well known, and a well-established historical experience, that war leads to debt, Dan Smith in his careful and detailed research demonstrates that the explosion of indebtedness itself also leads to the outbreak of war, and that in the process it not only gives the cycle a new twist, for wars do in fact lead to further indebtedness for all participants whether they 'win' or 'lose' the war, but imposes its burdens of violence, injury and death on the creditor economies too.[23]

It is not difficult for older generations of British to remember the massive debt which was the outcome of the Second World War. They will recognise well the popular feeling which was summed up in the bitter if understated comment from *The*

Economist of December 1945 which Smith quotes, 'It is rather aggravating to find that the reward for losing a quarter of the national wealth in the common cause is to pay tribute for half a century to those who have been enriched by the war.'[24] History abounds with examples of nations reduced to penury by a war, no matter whether they won or lost; most notable in our century is the process represented by the way in which the First World War led to indebtedness, to punitive reparations imposed on Germany, and through them in turn to one of the critical factors making the Nazi party's programme so attractive, and thereby leading again to war.

For the causal connections do in fact work in both directions. On the one hand, war involves huge expenditure, usually far more than a nation can spare, and therefore results in debt. Even before there is a war, preparations for war exact a heavy toll on government budgets. We need to remember, even as we use expressions like 'creditor country' and 'debtor country' as a convenient and indicative shorthand, that there is no country in the world as indebted, that is to say with as large a deficit, as the United States, and much of that is the result of inflated military expenditure. That to speak of the USA as a 'debtor' nation seems inappropriate is a good example of the phenomenon we observed when we were considering domestic debt, namely that the word 'debt' is only used when the issue of repayment becomes both imminent and a problem. But there is no doubt that one of the results of preparing for and waging war is indebtedness, sometimes on an enormous scale.

But as Smith also documents, the Gulf War is a singular example both of the role of debt in provoking war and of the management of debt as a strategic part of the waging of it. While the causes of a war are always varied and complex, there is little doubt that the refusal of other Arab states to refund to Iraq the $10 to $12 billion of indebtedness it had incurred in the long war with Iran was an important factor; for even when Iraq, after a month of Allied bombing, began to acknowledge the possibility of withdrawing from Kuwait, it still insisted in its statements that sums owed by Iraq to 'aggressor Gulf and foreign countries' should be forgiven.[25]

The power of debt was also evident in the way in which the USA exploited Egypt's indebtedness in order to secure its membership of the coalition against Iraq. It was able, on its own

account and by securing remissions by other states to which
Egypt was indebted, to reward Egypt for its participation in the
sum of between $20 and $25 billion, and at the same time to
secure some modification in the terms imposed by the IMF for
loans to Egypt. The indebtedness had come about to a considerable extent through the purchase of military equipment from the
USA in the first place. As Smith remarks, the other side of this
manipulation of indebtedness in the conduct of war was the
warning to Jordan that it could expect no more aid if it did not
join in on the anti-Iraq side. Yet Jordan turned out probably to
be among the worst hit of all through the Gulf War, with an
increase from 20 per cent to 30 per cent in the proportion of its
population living below the poverty line in the seven months
from August 1990.[26]

As with so many statistics, determining the number of deaths
in war with any accuracy is difficult and controversial – and
probably beside the point. There is endless scope for argument
about which casualties were due to war, and even what precisely
counts as a war. As Smith notes, having made the point that
somewhere around twenty million people have died in wars since
1945, and that probably five million people or so have died in
the (roughly) forty-eight wars which were being waged in the
world in January 1991, 'at this scale of carnage, a few thousand
deaths – even a few hundred thousand, truth to tell – do not
affect these necessarily rough estimates either way.'[27] Equally, the
details of conflicts and their causation vary from country to
country, and the relationship of debt to war can be argued about
in each case. What is sadly not open to much doubt is that debt
is a key result of war, and that it is also a source of war rather
than peace. 'Debt prepares the ground on which the seeds of
conflict fall, watering the martial crop as it grows.'[28] Mostly the
structure of credit and debt is such that the wars and the carnage
are held at a distance from the creditors and the powerful,
affecting principally the poorest of the world. But *caveat creditor*:
the cycle from debt to war and back again places the whole
world on a war footing, and therefore on a debt footing too.
The numbers may be smaller, but the death and suffering of
those involved in war will not for ever be held at a distance.

In any case what we have surveyed in this section is a terrify-
ingly interconnected set of developments and outcomes, which
cannot in principle be separated from each other. The war dead,

the millions of refugees and migrants, those reduced to hunger and homelessness, the ecosystems destroyed and plundered, the loss of democracy and independence, the distortions of trade and the competitive export of unemployment – these all feed off and in turn generate the money-and-power relationship we call credit and debt. Nobody can claim that if we solved the debt problem (assuming we knew how to and had the will to do so) we should thereby solve all the world's problems. But nobody should claim that the cycle of global suffering can be broken without attention to the debts we have encouraged, incurred and manipulated, and none should comfort themselves with the false belief that some attention to the debt crisis will not save some lives. And at that point lives – be they hundreds, thousands or perhaps we may hope millions – are not an inevitable statistical margin of error, but a critical test of our responsibility and commitment as citizens of the world. Once again, our question 'Who is Jesus Christ for us today?' speaks not just for victims but to humanity in its autonomous, economic strength.

6

Everything, even money, has a price

Slavery, debt and 'Christ for us today'

As it was profoundly difficult to write about domestic debt in Chapter 3, so it was to write about international debt in Chapter 5, and for similar reasons. For what we are talking about is nothing less than the progressive demeaning of more and more of the inhabitants of our world by a phenomenon that seems deeply intractable. Resistance to change comes not just from the complexities of the structures of world trade and the large profits to be made from lending money, but also from our sense that if change is to happen we shall have to be prepared to sacrifice – or at least give a far lower priority to – a principle that we have learned to live with and value, namely that debts should be repaid.

I have made the point before that our eyes have been constantly turned to the victims of this crisis, people who are being forced to endure a situation very similar to that created by the slave trade before it was abolished. Paul Spray lists three similarities between the slave trade and the debt crisis:

> First, they both have enormous human cost, and raise the same kind of fundamental moral issues. Second, they involve concerted campaigns, and the anti-slavery campaign is worth looking at because it succeeded. But thirdly, though the abolition of slavery was very important, it did not eliminate poverty or end unjust relations between Europe and America. In the same way, removing debt is vitally important, but it only lifts a constraint: at present, governments however committed to justice and supported by the people, have their policies severely restricted by the need to repay (or the consequences of not paying). Removing debt would lift that burden, but of course it does not ensure a just government at home, nor tackle other aspects of injustice between North and South.[1]

Because the slave trade now seems so repellent to us, it is hard to recall that it was itself grounded, in its day, in many of the same assumptions that now support the level of international debt, assumptions of moral rightness and economic necessity. At the heart of the slave trade lay convictions of racial superiority which served to justify social arrangements we now consider intolerable; it is worth recollecting that such arguments have continued to be advanced in this century with horrific consequences. Nor was it obvious to our forebears that there was any way of running an economy that did not depend on the existence of slaves. The attack on the moral and religious convictions about racial superiority succeeded only at the point where the economic justification for the maintenance of slavery also became untenable. In the end, as Olaudah Equiano, a slave brought from Africa in the eighteenth century, bravely prophesied, 'In a short Space of Time, One Sentiment alone will prevail, from Motives of Interest as well as Justice and Humanity.'[2]

His prophecy, and the connection between debt and slavery, can be found far earlier too, in the biblical record of the hope for liberation, and in a place where the tradition of evening recitation should have imprinted it on our minds. For generations Simeon's song, *Nunc Dimittis*, has been an inseparable part of the Church's evening repertoire, a fixture in whatever prayers were said last thing at night, and particularly in Compline and Evening Prayer.

Not only does Simeon's song belong to the evening of the day; it has also become associated with the evening of our years. Simeon's has been the paradigm of the holy death, welcomed in submission at the end of a life lived trusting in God's promises − now that all has been fulfilled it is time to be let go: 'Lord, now lettest thou thy servant depart in peace . . .'. And then, when the burial ritual is complete, the words are recited again as the coffin is borne from the Church. If the theologies and spiritualities of liberation have taken hold of the *Magnificat* in the service of a gospel of revolution, the *Nunc Dimittis* has come to belong to a more personal area of life, the universally human, the time of evening and of our dying when we most need resources of faith to calm and sustain us.

Yet there is in Simeon's words something more vibrant and demanding than that, perhaps more 'political' than the translations we have usually bring out. 'Now you are releasing your slave, Master, according to your word in peace', he says. The words 'master' and 'slave' used in relation to God might be a metaphor, but metaphors only work when they connect with an experience or at least a memory.

What suggests that this might indeed be an announcement of liberation is what we are told of the hope being sustained by Anna, the elderly woman who was in the Temple with Simeon: Anna's circle of friends had been waiting, we are told, 'for the liberation of Jerusalem'. Simeon, for his part, had lived his life in the expectation of the 'consolation of Israel', that remarkable promise of liberation uttered by the prophet of the exile, ' "Comfort, O comfort my people," says your God. "Speak tenderly to Jerusalem, and cry to her, that she has served her term." . . . "In the wilderness prepare the way of the Lord, make straight in the desert a highway for our God. Every valley shall be lifted up, and every mountain and hill be made low." '

'Now, Master, you are releasing your slave.' Looking as we do from the vantage point of hindsight, we wonder at the time it took for that release of slaves to take place, and for the promise Simeon saw to be fulfilled not just for his people but for the many nations of real slaves that history has seen. But even so we speak too soon. True it is – or at least officially so – that the trade in people, their capture and sale, has been abolished. But we must not be complacent yet about the abolition of many other features of slavery: people working for nothing except the barest subsistence; people labouring so that others may profit and deriving scarcely any reward from their labour themselves.

I remarked in Chapter 4 that as far as our biblical forebears were concerned, the aspect of the world economy we have been considering, debt, was the main reason why slavery came into being. Slaves in the Hebrew experience existed not by conquest and the iniquities of the slave trade of our modern history, but quite simply through debt. The conversation between Joseph and the starving people of the land (to which I referred earlier) is, after all, not that remote from those that governments have to have with the World Bank:

Now there was no food in all the land, for the famine was very severe . . . Joseph collected all the money to be found in the land of Egypt and the land of Canaan, in exchange for the grain that they bought; and Joseph brought the

money into Pharaoh's house. When the money from
the land of Egypt and from the land of Canaan was spent,
all the Egyptians came to Joseph, and said, 'Give us food!
Why should we die before your eyes? For our money is
gone.' And Joseph answered, 'Give me your livestock, and
I will give you food.' . . . When that year was ended, they
came to him the following year, and said to him, 'We
cannot hide from my lord that our money is all spent; and
the herds of cattle are my lord's. There is nothing left
in the sight of my lord but our bodies and our lands. . . .
We with our lands will become slaves to Pharaoh; just give
us seed so that we may live and not die.

(Genesis 47:13, 15–16, 18–20)

Certainly the transaction lacks the sophistication and economic complexity of a modern discussion about a structural
adjustment programme; but if you look at the power relations
there is little to choose: the effect of poverty is to make the
arrangement totally unequal in either case, and the outcomes
have great similarities. Basic to slavery is not being for yourself:
your existence is for your master and all you are and all you
produce is for your master's benefit, in discharge of the service
you 'owe' merely for the privilege of being kept alive. In the
light of the time it took for slavery to be abolished our question
has to be, how long will it take before the similar state of affairs
created by the debt crisis is brought to an end? What needs to
be done for Simeon's vision of a promised end to slavery in its
widest sense to be fulfilled and this aspect of Anna's hoped-for
liberation to come to pass?

Fortunately, what happens is not all in the hands of the
'donors'. Liberation theology is just one testimony to the fact
that there will always be among the hungry those who ask not
just *where* the next meal is coming from but *why* it isn't here. It
is a huge tribute to the human spirit that the poorest and
hungriest still include among them those who will not keep
quiet about those questions even if it is made clear that silence
is the price of food.

At the root of the international debt crisis there also lie convictions that have gone unquestioned too long about the 'only
possible' way to run a world economy, and at the same time
about the 'right' kind of society for people to live in. The

conviction about maintaining the rules of the market goes hand in hand with the view that industrialised and technological development represents the right way for the poorer nations of the world to improve their lot. We are accustomed to speak with certainty of the need to repay debts, and this is paralleled by the equal certainty with which those responsible for the regulation of the world economy convince themselves that that repayment will be accomplished by the continued application of the very models of development and trade which brought the debt crisis into being in the first place. It is indeed natural that George and Sabelli should introduce the language of 'faith' into their account of the World Bank,[3] for what faces us is a set of mutually supporting beliefs and economic arrangements which scarcely admit of any counter-evidence.

It took time to learn that the remedy required for slavery was not an amelioration of its conditions but the total end of the practice. For all the moral and religious support it had enjoyed, it had to be declared unacceptable as a model for human relations; the process of achieving an end to slavery involved all that we know of political campaigning, the forming of alliances and the gradual discovery of economic alternatives. We shall have to do the same in the case of debt if its dehumanising and destructive effects are to be brought to an end. In the next section we shall consider the attempts currently being made to secure some remission of debt, in particular towards the celebration of the 'Great Jubilee' in the year 2000. Here are attempts, pursued with similar realism and economic and political astuteness, and still against considerable odds, to make a difference, and thereby to achieve some improvement in the lot of the poor.

Yet these very campaigns for some realistic remission bring us face to face with a more radical concern still, which we shall need to pursue later. Our exploration of who Jesus Christ is for us today took us into the matter of indebtedness because this turns out to be a secular reality to which faith *must* speak if it is to make any sense. But Dietrich Bonhoeffer's demand was for something else too: for a way of speaking that did not only concern itself with humanity as victim or as weak, but that also addressed the strength that human beings claim to have acquired. Among such 'strengths' has been the conviction the powerful have about their running of a global economy that can operate apart from the claim of Christ. We must now look more closely at how that 'autonomous' global economy that seems so strong and so inevitable actually works. That is, if we are to know who Jesus Christ is for us today we must, when we have looked at what the possibilities for remission actually are, ask the further question, what has Christ to say to the strong voice of money?

The search for the Jubilee

> When we look at the debt question in the context of the Jubilee, we can see that the aim of the international community should not be simply the remission of debt, but that of removing the burdens which prevent the poorest countries from taking their place on an equitable basis alongside other countries. In the Jubilee perspective, debt should be forgiven in order to restore justice, equity and harmony, so that the poorest nations can make a fresh start, can truly turn a new page in their history.[4]

Fortunately we do see signs that the issue of world debt is being taken seriously, and faltering steps are being taken to consider how something may be done to alleviate it. The words of Cardinal Etchegaray seek to use the turn of the millennium as an opportunity to challenge the world to a new solidarity, a '*prophetia futuri*, a vision of future hope rooted in an understanding of God's original plan for his creation'. Such a visionary view of the inspiration which the turn of the millennium may offer has become more widespread, and campaigns have begun to use this 'jubilee' as the occasion for a serious step towards remission of at least those debts that seem beyond the bounds of repayment.

Campaigns for debt remission face two major practical dilemmas which, as we shall see in the next chapter, are not without parallel in the history of jubilee and of the controls on the lending of money at interest. They are well expressed by Martin Dent. The first difficulty, he says, is that any act of remission to take effect on a certain date will destroy any chance there might be of loans being offered in the period prior to it. His response, and that of JUBILEE 2000, is to distinguish the kinds of debt for which remission is sought from that for which it is not.

The debt which we seek to remit is not every penny owing on 31 December 1999, for such a plan would inhibit all lending in the years before the JUBILEE. Rather do we seek to remit the inert debt which has been built up from the exceptional years of the oil decade. . . . We are thus attacking not all debt, but inert debt up to the moment of remission. To take the analogy of the human stomach, we are not seeking to remove the food which goes through it day by day for digestion or expulsion, but rather things that have remained and festered in the stomach for many days and can only be removed by a special purge or an operation.[5]

The thought here is that defining the kind of debt for which remission is sought allows a reasonable chance of preventing necessary loans from drying up in the period between now and the date, the year 2000, when remission is granted. There is an element of rough justice here: a date will be selected (Dent suggests the beginning of 1993), and capital and accrued interest outstanding at that date will be deemed to have arisen from the petro-dollars of the 1980s. The assertion is that the debt that had accrued at that time was of a unique character; once forgiven, it will not recur. We have then to ask the question, what changes in the world financial system could accompany such an act of remission so as to ensure that there is no repetition?

But there is a second dilemma, too: the campaigns are encountering considerable resistance on the part of banks to any general writing off of debts on the grounds that it would undermine the principle that debts have to be repaid. I recall a similar point being made at a meeting of bishops called to consider this topic: would it not be better, a speaker asked, for the debtor nations to renege on their obligations rather than have them remitted, since in that way the sanctity of debt would be safeguarded? As a result of this view of the sanctity of debt it appears that the most likely way forward in practice will be a case by case consideration of the needs of particular countries. In the manner of applications for bankruptcy, where there is a genuine case that the burden of debt is clearly beyond repayment, an opportunity for a fresh start will be given and full repayment will not be required.

Such is the fear of precedent: cancel debt in any public and general way and loans will cease to be regarded as a matter of obligation. Leave it as a matter of individual supplication, and a gracious and forgiving response might be forthcoming; the poor will in the end be helped more by that means, not least because confidence in the general repayment of debt will be maintained, and therefore loans will continue to be offered. *Justice* will have been done in the sense that a principle of *mercy* will also have been followed, for it is an issue of justice that none should be reduced to penury and hopelessness, and that the power of the creditor should not be given free rein to destroy the life of the poor and powerless. In famous words from Shakespeare's *The Merchant of Venice*, '[Mercy] is an attribute of God himself, and earthly power doth then show likest God's, When mercy seasons justice.'[6]

Not surprisingly, this view is to be found repeatedly in the campaign literature asking for remission of debt, because it is in a sense the most realistically possible. It assumes that in the period between now and 2000 it would be possible to

> set a clear time-table for the completion of the process [of remission], and to make clear that having achieved this new level playing field in debt relations, future loans must be made and repaid in a more disciplined way and in an environment of fairer trading relations.[7]

Such a statement capitalises on the instincts of compassion that can be aroused when faced with disasters of the kind described in the last chapter, while at the same time having a note of firmness about the long-term changes that must accompany remission.

There are, however, other appeals to rather different aspects of the traditions of jubilee emerging at the present time. Some, for example, take seriously the *rhythmic* aspects of Sabbath and jubilee. This theme appears constantly in the papers given to the May 1996 Bossey consultation of Jewish and Christian biblical scholars on the subject of Sabbath and jubilee, hosted by the World Council of Churches.[8] There is indeed, as for instance Yolande Bernard states in his submission to the conference, much in such a concept of rhythm that would contribute to the health of an overworking industrialised world. For cultures that have come to exploit the environment and that have lost the capacity for communal celebration, there is much to commend such a rhythm, and much in the accumulated law and wisdom of Jews and Christians that points in that direction.

However, when it comes to the particular matter of the release of debt, Paul Spray's submission to that conference, 'Five areas for jubilee today', builds on this notion of rhythm in a very important way: the Sabbath and jubilee traditions do indeed involve *regular* occasions for interrupting the natural course of human social systems, with their inevitable tendency to corruption and exploitation. Seeing a campaign for the remission of debt in this way, as the creation of a 'structure of interruption', assists in meeting two general difficulties about the application of the jubilee tradition in our time. First, it avoids the suggestion that the whole idea is utopian, an attempt to construct a totally new economic order with little real chance of acceptance, something purely visionary. Secondly, it also avoids the related suggestion that an act of remission of this kind will then never have to be asked for again, that the remission will have been a once-for-all liberation from unrepayable debt, one that will never recur. It does not therefore seek to ground remission in the desperation of individual countries; or their membership, conferred by the judges of the international financial community, of some implied category of the 'deserving poor' whose past misfortunes or present better intentions might be thought of as the 'justification' for the remission they are to receive. Rather, such reasoning bases jubilee in the structure of things, as a recurrent human need in the context of the corruptibility of human endeavour.

Susan George for her part does not mention the possibility of jubilee of any kind or root her proposals in that tradition. Her proposals contain more than a little suspicion about all dramatic proposals for debt remission, which she suspects strongly either will not happen at all or, if they do, will simply serve to bolster the kind of development model currently favoured by the IMF and World Bank and the small, self-serving élites which currently control debtor countries and which benefit from the loans that have been provided – and, indeed, which would most likely benefit again from any acts of remission. Her own proposals are hard-headed, demanding and holistic. Her '3-D solution – debt, development, democracy'[9] certainly embodies an element of remission, which she calls 'creative reimbursement', allowing debtor countries to 'reimburse' by undertaking democratically accountable development programmes, paid for in their own currencies or 'repaid' in kind by, for instance, devoting local resources to preserving their own natural heritage. But what she asks for is not simply a once-for-all write-off or the continued process of bailing out the banks, but the making of alliances with debtor countries and their people so as to insist that programmes are undertaken for the benefit of their own populations. She is well aware of the long process for which she is asking, but convinced that it is the only way to solve the debt crisis. Her call is indeed reminiscent of Cardinal Etchegaray's demand that 'the aim of the international community should not be simply the remission of debt, but that of removing the burdens which prevent the poorest countries from taking their place on an equitable basis alongside other countries.'

Without going into such detail, Michael Taylor also suggests that most attempts at jubilee are likely to be more a question of 'inching forward' than of making an 'imaginative leap'. Even so, he says, the idea of jubilee

> has often been dismissed for never having been put into practice and being unlikely to come about. It is written off as an unhelpful, utopian concept. There are good reasons for doing so. Many proposals for jubilee are unrealistic. They simply would not work. The evidence of lasting progress in overcoming poverty and injustice is slight. The teachings of Christian faith itself insist that the kingdom, though present and growing within our history, will be fully realised only beyond it. At best, jubilee, like love, is impossible possibility. It is always there to question our self-satisfied achievements and call us on to new heights. It is highly useful as a goad, but never realizable.[10]

This is a 'realism' of a wholly different order, not just political but also theological. Like the understanding of jubilee as a *recurrent* need it is grounded in a true perception of the character of humankind and of all systems of authority that human beings are able to generate. Such a theological realism is crucial both to a diagnosis of how the debt trap affects people, domestically and internationally, and to recognising the root causes of this crisis.

The power of money

> Because wealth in money is the easiest kind of wealth to
> ascertain, it becomes the standard by which every kind of
> wealth is judged; and the possession of money becomes the
> ideal of the majority of people. As a result the evaluation
> of social relationships is shifted from the realm of the per-
> sonal to that of the impersonal, the chaotic. The
> senselessness of the lottery on the small scale is repeated at
> a global level in the economic crises which throw millions
> out of work, and precipitate wars. The unbelievable conse-
> quences of inflation and of currency reform have made the
> chaotic character of the monetary system abundantly clear;
> and again and again the nonsense of economics renders
> illusory all that has been gained by the good sense of tech-
> nology.[11]

Theodor Bovet's pastoral handbook was written in 1951, and the
characteristics of money to which he draws attention there have
become even more pronounced in the decades since. Its possession of an 'impersonal, purely quantitative and potential
character'[12] means that unlike other possessions it does not confer
responsibilities on its holder – those who own houses have to
paint them, and those who have farms have to tend their fields
and their flocks – but instead confers pure power to be turned
into whatever its owner wishes, for its only distinctive feature is
that it carries a number which determines its purchasing power,
a power that is 'a potential and invisible power, ready for action
at all times, and able to assume every possible form'. That is
what gives it its almost religious power; as Bovet remarks, money
is 'officially minted *mana*' which in turn makes it for us 'a
standing temptation straight from Chaos, the Anti-Being, and
the devil.'[13]

In speaking in this way, Bovet is capturing the essence of the
comment of Georg Simmel in his magisterial work on *The
Philosophy of Money*, in which he compares the power of God
and the power of money in modern society.

> The essence of the notion of God is that all diversities and
> contradictions in the world achieve a unity in him. . . .
> Out of this idea, that in him all estrangements and all
> irreconcilables find their unity and equalization, there arises

the peace, the security, the all-embracing wealth of feeling that reverberate with the notion of God which we hold.

There is no doubt that, in their realm, the feelings that money excites possess a psychological similarity with this. In so far as money becomes the absolutely commensurate expression and equivalent of all values, it rises to abstract heights way above the whole broad diversity of objects.[14]

The feelings which Simmel describes – and whose effect on the character of a person, as Bovet warns, reflect themselves also in the priorities of a whole society – are related closely to all that has been said hitherto about the operation, nationally and internationally, of the credit and debt economy. For example, recently, just at the time that the Archbishop of Canterbury was asking for a debate on the ethical basis of our society, and asking for schools to assume a key role in inducting our children into it, schools were faced with another proposal: that they should raise money by selling advertising space on their premises. It was a sad and revealing coincidence.

We might wish schools to be places where students can appropriate for themselves the vision of what it is to be human and where they can enter into our ethical and spiritual inheritance. What the advertising proposal showed (rather starkly, though we surely knew it already) was that there is an altogether different 'moral basis' making its demands felt on our educational institutions. If we seek to get a moral debate going, it is that moral basis we shall need to challenge. If we want schools and colleges to be places of learning, or for that matter if we want hospitals to be places of healing, we shall have to find ways of confronting some of those 'other influences' of which the Archbishop spoke. They affect our children not only when they are out of school; they invade schools and our other vital institutions all the time. Chief among those other influences is the ever increasing power and authority of money. Apparently in the minds of some it is never too early for children to learn to become its disciples, to learn that to be a citizen now is first and foremost to spend money.

The political rhetoric of recent decades has all been about an increase of choice; not surprisingly that leads to the idea that we choose what standards to apply in the whole of life. But in fact we have become more and more obsessed with the cash nexus

and with the power of money as the criterion of value. More and
more pages of our newspapers are devoted to helping those who
have money to manage it so as to make it make more; even the
very poorest are required, through the social fund, to involve
themselves in the borrowing of money; and, as we have noted
before, anyone starting a university course knows that even if
she fails to gain a degree, she can be sure of ending up with a
debt. In many sectors the most significant profit to be made from
manufacturing something is generated by lending the money to
someone to buy it.

As we are encouraged to make our own provision for our
pensions, more and more people will spend more and more time
checking their future by looking at the financial pages of the
newspaper, in addition to seeing what has happened to the value
of their house. For as is only to be expected of a god – and Our
Lord identified money as a god – money has its own 'spiritual
reading', its own demands for time and energy, and a constant
thirst for sacrifices. Like all gods, it seeks the constant increase
of its territory, so that it determines more and more of the life
choices we make. Like all gods, and unlike the Father of Jesus
Christ, it produces its included ones and its excluded ones, in
this case the haves and the have-nots, and claims to determine
human worth by its own simple standard. We may imagine all
the while that we live in a confusing world in which we all have
to determine our own ethical basis for living; in fact there is a
far graver reality which is the constraining of our choices by the
'objective standard' of financial value that presses upon us from
all sides.

I do not underestimate either the difficulty or the importance
of the intellectual task of establishing a credible moral basis for
our life together as a society and as a world; and it is a task
which people of faith, not least Christian faith, are called to
undertake. But we need to understand that we are not moving
in on empty territory. Rather it is a territory already possessed
by a divinity that is exacting its own demands, presenting itself
as credible beyond question, objectively verifiable, and utterly
totalitarian – 'there is no alternative'. It claims the allegiance of
the most powerful in the land, is supported with few reservations
by all political parties (how else will they get votes?), and can
furnish itself with almost unlimited weaponry for its own
defence. It dangles before our eyes the hope – its eschatology –

of growth in personal wealth, whether through the constant news of ever-increasing top salaries or the offer of a once-for-all liberation through a win on the National Lottery. Meanwhile, as we have seen in the statistics and the stories of the operation of the economy of credit and debt, it sets about depriving the poorest of their future, and all the other destructions to which Susan George has so eloquently referred.

What has happened, in ways that our ordinary dealings with money prevent us from realising, is the divorce of money from anything we normally understand by the way the real world functions. Only occasionally, when something goes wrong, do we find ourselves asking fundamental questions, and feeling as we do so that we are sounding foolish. At a meeting held to enable people to consider the implications of the loss by the Church Commissioners of some £800 million through unsuccessful investment in property, those present were all given a careful explanation of the course of events that had led up to the loss. The explanation sounded clear and coherent enough, until someone in the audience, with what was almost a note of apology for asking a foolish question, asked, 'If they have lost £800 million, who's got it?' Carefully, the answer was explained: it was not like that; it was as if a house you owned and thought worth a certain sum turned out to be worth several thousand pounds less. You were poorer, but nobody else actually had the money. This prompted me to raise the question then, and now with far more urgency, 'Suppose instead of losing that money they had gained it; first of all, we would not be holding this meeting because we wouldn't be worried about it; but secondly, would we think of asking the question, "If they've gained the money, who's lost it?" '

The last chapter makes it very clear where the losses in such transactions ultimately land: on those who are at the losing end of the market, those whose civil liberties disappear, whose children are not educated or even fed, those who end up working for low wages in poor economies or have to turn to the market in drugs. Yet we do not notice that this is happening because we are not at that end of the market. We therefore consent to the myth that there need be no losers in the money game, provided only that it is wisely conducted in a supervised way. There were indeed serious shortcomings in the way in which the business of the Church Commissioners was being managed, and much energy has been expended in correcting those faults, principally in accountability.

But this does not meet the real issue thrown up by an event of that kind. What we are faced with there is the setting free of money, not just in the sense of the deregulation of the institutions which manage it, but also in the sense of its being cut loose from the real economy where goods and services are exchanged. When that happens, as it has, money, with its promise of freedom, is itself given such freedom that it destroys the very freedom it pretends to offer. The sociologist Nigel Dodd describes such a 'mature money economy', himself quoting Simmel:

> In the mature money economy, money's empowering features have compromised that very freedom which money itself promises to embrace. Monetary freedom has in this sense been alienating. It is a freedom which is empty of content, having only negative connotations linked to the removal of constraint: 'In itself, freedom is an empty form which becomes effective, alive and valuable only through the development of other life-contents.'[15] These life-contents will be stunted whenever money is treated as an end in itself. This is exactly what has happened in modern society. Money, as the ultimate economic instrument, has been turned into the ultimate economic goal. It has imploded in on itself as Mammon.[16]

A far more dramatic illustration of this process occurred in the recent collapse of Barings, the international bank, and I recall the sense of revelation when it was brought out into the open. I was watching a *Panorama* programme, which sought to convey something of the history that led up to the collapse of Barings. Nick Leeson, their trader in Singapore, had incurred monumental losses; how, the presenter (and the viewers) wanted to know, had this come about? Carefully, in the language of someone explaining the obvious to a rather slow pupil, the Japanese banker explained that Leeson had borrowed money and invested it in the expectation of a rise in the Tokyo stock exchange. 'That rise did not happen,' said the banker; 'so he decided to try and raise it himself.' The presenter looked as dumbfounded as I felt.

We were indeed dumbfounded: one person, or one firm, singlehandedly raising the Japanese stock exchange? The pre-

senter put to the banker the question that was surely in all
viewers' minds: did Leeson really believe that? Had he taken
leave of his senses? The banker smiled: 'Not at all,' he said; 'he
had done it before. All that defeated him at this time was the
earthquake.' What we were being told was that there was a
'virtual' economy, one in which money could work with itself
and for itself, without any apparent connection with the world
of trade, *and could do so quite successfully* nearly all of the time (for
who knows or cares about the effects of that economy on the
world's poor?). For the real economy to interrupt the processes
of that virtual economy took nothing short of an earthquake.

I do not – I need hardly say – believe in a God who sends
earthquakes, with all the human suffering and devastation they
cause, in order to teach errant human financiers a lesson. But at
the point when that sentence was uttered by a banker, I did
believe that we should do well to take extremely seriously a
situation in which reality is powerless to make an impression on
a very costly kind of unreality unless something as devastating as
an earthquake interrupts our daydream and recalls us from the
world of money that has 'imploded upon itself as Mammon'.

As we shall see, it is this imploding character of money as it
has become that is at the root of the destructive power of the
huge growth in domestic and international credit and debt. For
of all the ways of making money, making money out of money
has become by far the most profitable. Ulrich Duchrow points
out that in the twenty years between 1970 and 1990, Germany's
real gross national product had increased by about one-and-a-
half times; wages by just under three times; but earnings from
interest, that is money made out of money, by nearly seven
times.[17] What, we must ask ourselves, does this money made out
of money represent?

For some, not least for some who write from a specifically
Christian standpoint, the answer to this question is clear, and
comforting. It is simply the case that money is like any other
commodity in commanding a price in the market. The price of
money, like the price of anything else, is the result of individuals
doing what they choose to do with their resources: buying,
selling, earning, saving, spending, giving, lending, borrowing. It
is the working out in practice of what in the view of some is
the strongest moral element in Christianity, which

does not just teach that all improvements in social and economic arrangements are worthless without courageous, kind and selfless individuals to put the new systems into practice. It also teaches that the individual is *the only proper moral end* of all human thought and action, including politics.[18]

The market economy debate

This is not the place in which to engage in yet another to add to the many critiques of individualism, except perhaps to ask for at least a passing look at the millions of 'individuals' who have statistically and in their personal stories of debt and impoverishment been occupying our attention in the chapters on domestic and individual debt. We might wonder whether they have any justification for believing that they are being treated as 'the only proper moral end of all human thought and action, including politics'. If they are, and if it is clear that economic systems are being operated in a way that operates to their continuing and accelerating disadvantage, how are those individuals who are responsible for their operation demonstrating the 'courageous, kind and selfless' qualities which are needed?

Certainly the market economy has received robust and wide-ranging theological defence, perhaps most of all in the writing of Michael Novak, in particular his *The Spirit of Democratic Capitalism*.[19] He sees in democratic capitalism the most creative opportunity for the poor to improve their standard of living, and in the free market the greatest possibilities of enterprise and creativity, and therefore of the living out of the image of God in each person. Behind the poverty of Latin America lie not the policies of democratic capitalist nations, but the socialist preoccupations of the Latin American countries themselves.

Particularly important for our purposes is Novak's argument about the place of money in capitalism. Capital is not, he says, money alone; capital is 'money taken from idleness and made active through practical intelligence', in which biblical faith encourages us to trust.[20] Through that exercise of the human *caput*, money became *capital*, no longer part of a 'zero-sum' game in which what a miser hoarded was thereby subtracted from the common store of available resource. Markets reward, and therefore encourage, ingenuity, and they have an inherent interest in the many, thereby restraining the power of élites. In an example that reveals more than he seems to realise, he points out that whereas ownership of a coach and horses was confined to the very few, the motor car is now a mass means of transportation.[21] What the market rewards it is also clearly showing itself unable to restrain, and it must surely be doubted whether a system that produces exponential growth in car use can possibly serve the future of humankind well.

With such robust support for capitalism, it is not surprising that Novak has none of the concerns about the place of money that we noticed earlier in Bovet. There is nothing particular, or particularly dangerous, about money or the pursuit of it.

> Among the things for which human beings compete, money is neutral and may be used in wise stewardship or foolish. Since it is impersonal and instrumental, its possessors may accept it with an infinite range of human attitudes and use it for a vast range of choices. More to the point, those who have money are obliged by it to become careful stewards, under pain of losing it or cutting foolishly into their capital. Their natural interest lies in investing it soundly and well. This interest leads them to produce more of it than there was in the first place. Thus a money economy is inherently dynamic.[22]

There are some revealing phrases here, notably the suggestion that money creates obligations – we may say debt – which turn out, however, to be obligations to itself. It has indeed a 'life of its own' which means that it has a capacity to become more than an instrument of exchange. He is also clear that money wisely invested produces more of itself, and that this is not at anyone else's expense.

Confronted with criticisms of the effect of the market left to itself, Novak always raises the question whether other systems perform better, and finds that they do not. So for example in response to Ronald Preston's complaint that markets left to themselves produce 'cumulative inequalities of income which distort the market by drawing the relatively scarce resources to what the wealthy want and away from the necessities of the

poor',[23] Novak asserts that other systems, whether pre-capitalist
or socialist, do worse in this respect, and in any case the condition
of the poor today is far improved over what it was, say, in 1892
(or 1932) so that 'the very word "necessities" now entails far
higher standards than in centuries past – far above mere survival
or subsistence'.[24]

Consistently Novak avoids the possibility that there are disastrous consequences to the present-day working of markets,
constantly claiming, as Richard Roberts observes, that his argument can be universalised when in fact he draws only on the
positive experiences that have emerged in very particular con-
texts.[25] Positive experiences are evidence of the operation of the
free market, negative ones can either be ignored or treated as
signs that the operation of the market has not been allowed to
be free. Perhaps the most blatant example of this is Novak's use
of the fact of increasing migration towards the countries of free
market economies as a sign of their success, while not mentioning
the human cost involved in such migration, both to those whose
migration is as likely to be the result of compulsion as of choice,
and to those who are left behind, themselves deprived by such
forced departures from their communities.[26]

The majority of those who have written about the operation
of the market from a theological standpoint have not done so
with Novak's robust confidence. Generally, like Preston, they
find the market, and the operation of capitalism in general, a
more ambiguous phenomenon. Richard Harries sets out a very
nuanced picture of the consequences of a market economy, and
in *Is there a Gospel for the Rich*? sets out both the advantages
and disadvantages of it and an ethic and spirituality for life within
it. He speaks for many in articulating the shape of a hesitant
and uneasy support for a system to which there seems no real
alternative.

> This [unease] arises not simply because of the contrast
> between our own comfortable lives and the abject misery
> of so many millions but also because many of the attitudes of
> the capitalist world seem to strike at the heart of our
> understanding of the Christian faith. A market economy
> takes it for granted that self-interest, competition and success
> in worldly matters are essential features of life.

And these need not be wholly bad, because

there is a basic congruity between the Christian faith and a free market. Nevertheless, certain characteristics of the capitalist system as we know it in practice are certainly inimical to Christian faith, and it is quite right that we should be sensitive to this and alive to the contradictions that it presents to our value system.[27]

Peter Sedgwick finds much in 'the enterprise culture' to affirm and cherish, while insisting that 'consuming and possessing without limit can be seen as a form of pathology',[28] asserting also that the power of the free market can be overwhelming and that therefore there is a requirement 'not to let the market rule our imagination, but to create new understandings of work and enterprise that are sustainable in this fragile world'.[29] John Atherton examines what he describes the 'conservative', 'liberal' and 'radical' responses Christian theologians have made to the operation of the market, believing that Christian social thought will develop only as it enters into the working of the market and the challenges to it.[30]

Money's life of its own

The general debate about whether we should or should not live in a market economy will doubtless go on, and while it goes on so will the market. But its very generality, together with the ease with which the struggle is given up in the face of the apparent political reality that there is no visible alternative in prospect, should leave us uneasy. For the word 'market' is operating here as a metaphor. The fruit and vegetable market I regularly patronise is a friendly and manageable place where nobody, so far as I can tell, has an unacceptable monopoly of supplies, nor is there any buyer who has cornered the whole market and excluded others from obtaining the produce they need. Once the word 'market' comes to be used to describe the vast electronic markets in which money and bonds are traded, let alone the whole economic system, we are in danger of being comforted by ideas that we carry over from the markets we know into areas that are fundamentally different in the way they work.

This is particularly true of the operation of the market in money. For once we speak in this way, that which was conceived as the instrument of exchange that enables us to participate in the market – for vegetables, coffee or whatever – has become itself a traded commodity. Many see this as inevitable, something no developed economy could do without. Preston makes the following optimistic assessment:

> There seems no reason why there should not be a market for money. Financial markets are not zero-sum games in which what one gains another loses. Properly run, they lead to general benefits in trading in goods and services, in trading in risks and liquidity, and in providing financial services.[31]

Similarly Stephen Green, himself a senior executive in an international banking group, affirms the necessity of that world and indeed of Christians like himself working within it. He is well aware of the inequalities and distortions that arise within it, but in the end agrees with George Carey, the Archbishop of Canterbury, that 'it is impossible to conceive of an advanced economy without a sophisticated financial sector'.[32] It is impossible to quote such remarks without remembering the words cited in our examination of domestic debt about the painful consequences of the road away from the piggy bank to the world of financial sophistication.

We are faced then with an apparently irresistible set of arguments in favour of a market in money: it produces benefits; we cannot do without it; all attempts at alternative systems have failed. Yet we must remind ourselves why it is that we are considering money at all: it is that what is taking place at the moment, and shows no sign of stopping, is a progressive enslavement to an economy of credit and debt which is itself reducing the poorest nations and the poor of our own society to destitution. The example of the motor car, used by Novak and quoted above, is in fact instructive. There is not much point in disputing the statement that we cannot do without the motor car. It is indeed hard to imagine human society without it. But we also know that when the statement is made it is always in furtherance of some further concession to the motor vehicle; behind the person making the statement there is a bulldozer not far away, ready to produce further miles of tarmac.

In fact the statement that 'we cannot do without the motor car' tells us nothing about how many cars we need or should find space for, what controls should be placed upon their use, or indeed whether there are not in fact communities or individuals who could and should manage without cars, or would profit from doing so. The statement that 'we need markets' likewise does not tell us anything about what kind of markets we need, where they should be and to what controls they should be subject. It is perfectly coherent to suggest that we need markets in some things and not in others; or that certain markets require special controls on their operation. Equally, the statement that 'an "advanced economy" needs money and bond markets and a financial services sector' does not of itself support the notion that the wave of deregulation which has become the economic orthodoxy of recent decades is in anybody's interest.

The seriousness of what happens when money takes on a life of its own and becomes a self-generating commodity in this way is further illustrated by the effect we can see on the traditional power of the nation state. For as Nigel Dodd shows in his *The Sociology of Money*,[33] it is not possible to consider money without noticing its effect on all aspects of culture, especially on the authority of the state which traditionally has been the authority that issues and validates money. The events surrounding Britain's departure from the European exchange rate mechanism are ample illustration of the impotence of modern national governments against the power of money when it has a life of its own and is traded in markets as though it were a commodity. Dodd remarks that the application to money of the concept of 'the market' is largely the result of, and in turn responsible for, much muddled thinking.

It is for precisely this reason that debates over [the European Single Currency] seem rarely to rise above the level of bluster and fancy where the loss of sovereignty is concerned. Geopolitical boundaries in relation to monetary networks have not completely disappeared. But they were never entirely secure in the first place. Confusion over the nature and importance of monetary sovereignty stems from a misconception of the characteristics of financial and monetary networks as markets. It is not at all clear that international monetary networks mark the emergence . . . of a market stretching across geopolitical boundaries whose operation approximates more and more closely to a perfection derived from economic reasoning. The very concept of the market, perfect or otherwise, is deeply problematical when examined closely.[34]

We may add, in the light of what we have seen happening to the world of credit and debt, that it is clearly not in some people's interests to let that concept be examined too closely.

For what has been happening is not in fact 'the operation of a free market in money', but rather the widespread use of interest rates, the last remaining instrument of government economic action, to deal with what is seen as the principal public enemy, inflation. Naturally the rampant inflations of such economies as Germany in the 1920s have left scars on the memory, and most people would want to direct policy towards making sure such inflation never happens again. Indeed at one time there was the hope in the USA, as J. K. Galbraith describes it, that by fierce regulation of the money supply inflation could become 'a thing that, once exorcised, would be gone forever'.[35] But that hope failed, basically because the political consequences were too great. Equally in the UK, the initial belief of the New Right was that provided some version of the money supply was kept constant, the market would ensure by a 'competitive equilibrium' that prices would remain constant. Will Hutton describes this belief as resting on a number of impossible assumptions, with which I agree, and therefore that it should be described as 'a piece of theology' – with which, of course, I do not![36]

But more recently, the use of interest rates for that purpose has had some very severe consequences, some of which we have already described. Of course it does not hurt those with money; as Galbraith remarks, higher interest rates, it is hoped, 'will curb inflation; in any case, they will not threaten men and women of good fortune. Those with money to lend, the economically well-endowed *rentier* class, will thus be rewarded.'[37] Questions about the effect on the poor are answered by reference to the trickle-down theory whereby what benefits the best off will eventually benefit the worst off too; in the light of what we have observed about the debt crisis, the poor can be forgiven for asking how long this might take.[38] Will Hutton for his part in his *The State We're In* not only describes in whose interests this theory operates, but reveals the way in which the priority of money and short-term gains is preventing the long-term satisfaction of the needs of the economy for investment; that state of affairs he believes requires radical thinking not just about the economy but about issues of governance and the constitution as well.[39]

These comments of Galbraith and Hutton illustrate why, although the raising of interest rates is the weapon against inflation chosen by those who profit by it, it is also clear that as a method it cannot finally work. John Turmel, a Canadian civil engineer and campaigner against usury, has in two long articles brought algebra, plumbing and poetry to bear on the task of demonstrating that the move from the piggy bank is not simply a move to greater sophistication, as it was earlier described, but a move towards allowing the money supply, and therefore the amount of credit and debt, to grow inexorably and exponentially. For banks do not lend out their depositors' money; they create new money through the financial instruments, various kinds of loans, which they are able to issue in proportion to their deposit base. That is the process that operated so clearly, and disastrously, during the late 1980s, and that will continue to operate into the future, if perhaps less spectacularly. For during that period, in the context of a rhetoric about restraining public borrowing and the nation paying its way, private credit exploded – and the more interest rates are raised, the more it will explode.[40]

Not surprisingly, those anxious to 'roll back' the power of the state view such developments with enthusiasm. Friedrich von Hayek, one of the leading protagonists of the freedom of the market, advocates the 'denationalisation of money', the abandonment of governments' monopoly over the issuing of currency.[41] In fact of course Dodd's observations above about the operation of the 'money markets' mean that this kind of government monopoly over the issuing of money has already become a very qualified reality, even if the politics of the relationship of the UK to Europe means that the rhetoric of monetary sovereignty is still loudly proclaimed. As a recent series of radio programmes graphically described, the links between currency and feelings of national identity remain very strong and are a powerful political reality affecting the policies of governments; but there is a widespread, if not always admitted, recognition that the nation-state is no longer able to be the defender of its own currency, and that alliances are therefore an absolute necessity.[42]

But alliances with whom and for what? If we find ourselves

in a world of global monetary transactions in which nation-states can exercise only limited, and apparently diminishing, control, states are likely to form defensive and competitive alliances to protect their domestic policies from the effects of financial speculation. Such is the way of the world. In the end only very large currency blocks will be able to exercise any control over the movement of money, and only if they are able to do that shall we be able to have a world in which the poorest do not find themselves facing what they are facing now, an inexorably rising quantity of debt, vulnerable to whatever competitive increases in interest rates they have to accept. Within the current organisation of international finances, therefore, the ultimate hope must lie in seeking groupings of nations that include, and give a real voice to, the poorest.

Both Timothy Gorringe in his *Capital and the Kingdom*[43] and Ulrich Duchrow in his *Alternatives to Global Capitalism*[44] take what John Atherton would call the 'radical' view of the development of the capitalist market system we have been considering: it is, they would both say, a way that leads, and is leading, to death. That causes them to doubt whether any arrangements are possible within it that can really improve the lot of the poor. It leads them further to believe that the Church in its own life must lead a radical disavowal of those methods and mechanisms that have brought the world of finance to where it currently finds itself (and where, they would say, it was bound to find itself). The requirement is the kind of alliance in support of the poor that Duchrow calls a 'networked, global, economic civil rights movement.'[45] It requires all those who have political rights and possibilities left to them in a world where power is overwhelmingly exercised by money to seek with others the extension of those possibilities by common and concerted action.[46]

For Gorringe (as also for Duchrow), 'the redemption of money will involve the abolition of usury'.[47] This is a challenge that takes us well beyond single acts of remission by the year 2000 or whenever, well beyond minor adjustments, to the way money works in an essentially capitalist framework. It takes us well beyond those proposals for an individual discipleship that involves detachment from money, beyond even a more serious concern with stewardship[48] or whatever; these may well be required of us in the pursuit of greater justice, but if we are not engaged in the fundamental task of redeeming money altogether, these acts of personal discipline and responsibility do no more than collude with the way of death that we have seen the economy of credit and debt has become.

Conclusion: 'Who is Jesus Christ for us today?'

The question of Christ turned out, in our discussion of Bonhoeffer, to entail the three linked questions of deciding who we are (the question of identity), who 'us' is (the question of solidarity), and whose 'today' it is to be (the challenge of discernment). We find ourselves after these chapters on the working of the credit and debt economy with data before our eyes that raise these three questions in a particularly sharp and insistent form.

Who is Christ and who are we? Consumer? Depositor? Usurer? Debtor? Where, that is to say, do we place ourselves and where do we place Christ in the international networks whose effects we have had to consider? For some, clearly, Christ is where we are, exercising the freedom that those who have money enjoy to do what they will with their own. The Christ of this selective freedom enjoys the choices and responsibilities that the world of money provides for those who have it, seeking within that to exercise as much compassion as he can without at any point confronting the results of the exercise of that freedom in the lives of those who have nothing. Or is Christ where they are, the ally of the penniless and the indebted? And in that case, what is his word and where do his actions lead? Surely in a direction that meets Bonhoeffer's challenges of an engagement with the world in its secularity and its strength, of a word and actions that do not accept the unacceptable, that choose the way that leads to life rather than the one that leads to death.

The question of 'us' raises again the limits of our solidarity. We have seen money as having a power to render ineffective many of the inherited loyalties, the patriotism and the national pride, that are the assumptions behind many of our constitutional mechanisms. That is, we have seen that money bestrides the world, uncontrollable as it seems by national powers. But we have seen also that it creates its own network and its own solidarity that claims the allegiance of us all if we will give it: all consumers, all investors, all creditors, all debtors, with our futures and those of our children mortgaged to a power greater than ourselves or our nations. In such a world what would it mean to discover new solidarities that might truly benefit the penniless and the bankrupt?

Above all, though, we have to ask about our commitment to 'today', and to the today of those for whom it may be the last. Unlike the strong in the world of the market, most of the world's people cannot bank on a future income, for the future is being devoured already by the market and the way it works. They cannot look to future profit, for that only comes to those who have today's riches to invest, and who by doing so claim in advance the harvest that the future will yield. Christ's question is, whose 'today' concerns you?

In examining the world of money we have seen clear signs of the way in which it operates and the character of its effects. We shall notice in the coming pages that the inheritance of faith, coming to birth in a world very different from this, nevertheless has its wisdom and its word to offer to the questions our world is raising for us. We shall notice too that the questions raised by the world of money spread themselves, like *mana*, through all our human transactions and relationships. It is not a power we can simply ignore in order to get on with living those parts of our lives where we fancy money does not hold sway; for as we shall see its language, its culture and the attitudes it spreads have already claimed much more of our lives and our concerns than we generally own. So if we would ask who Jesus Christ is for us today we must not leave this world of money out of account; for, as earlier we heard Dietrich Bonhoeffer say to the congregation in Barcelona, 'If we wish to have him, then he demands the right to say something decisive about our entire life.'

Forgotten wisdom

Thou shalt not give thy brother thy money for usury; and thou shalt not give him thy food for increase (Leviticus 25:37). There is the simple law for all of us; one of those which Christ assuredly came not to destroy, but to fulfill: and there is no national prosperity to be had but in obedience to it. How we usurers are to live, with the hope of our gains gone, is precisely the old Temple of Diana question. How Robin Hood or Cocur de Lion were to live without arrow or axe, would have been as strange a question to them, in their day. And there are many amiable persons who will not directly see their way, any more than I do myself, to an honest life; only, let us be sure that this we are leading now is a dishonest one.[1]

History does not record what the Treasurer of the City of New York thought when he was faced with the arrival of a rather unusual letter from Dorothy Day, Editor of *The Catholic Worker*, in July 1960. It was very much in accord with the views of John Ruskin above. *The Catholic Worker* was returning a cheque for the interest on the price of a property which they had used as a community house for the poor and which had been compulsorily purchased (they saw it as confiscation) from them. For the delay of eighteen months in paying the sum due interest had been awarded, and Dorothy Day was returning it 'because we do not believe in "money-lending" at interest'. Whatever the Treasurer thought, the accompanying letter enabled the files of the City to hold some robust and clear teaching on the matter.

As Catholics we are acquainted with the early teaching of the Church. All the early councils forbade it, declaring it reprehensible to make money by lending it out at interest. Canon law of the middle ages forbade it and in various decrees ordered that profit so obtained was to be restored. In the Christian emphasis on the duty of charity, we are commanded to lend gratuitously, to give freely, even in the case of confiscation, as in our own case – not to resist but to accept cheerfully.[2]

Day makes the point that in so far as the capital sum was used for good works, *The Catholic Worker* was happy that it should be so used without charge; while in so far as the money had been used for the salaries of those who had condemned people to jail, and 'for prisons, and the execution chamber at Sing Sing and for the executioner's salary, we can only protest the use of our money and turn with utter horror from taking interest on it'. She concludes by stressing that they are not judging individuals but 'trying to make a judgement on the *system* under which we live and with which we admit that we ourselves compromise daily in many small ways, but which we try and wish to withdraw from as much as possible.'[3]

Such a sustained argument against all forms of usury is offered also by Timothy Gorringe (whose position Stephen Green describes as 'extreme', a description which in relation to the mainstream position of churches at large is probably accurate).[4] On the basis of his account of the biblical and historical material, as well as of the effects of usury on the life of the contemporary world, Gorringe's judgement is uncompromising:

The redemption of money will involve – as Deuteronomy, the medieval theologians, and Luther all insisted – the abolition of usury. The charging of interest . . . involves a significant transfer of wealth to the richest groups of a country's population. This systematic transfer of money from those who need it most to those who need it least is one of the factors pushing the world towards catastrophe. It fuels the urge of the very rich, including the huge industrial and financial corporations, to compete with one another purely for the sake of economic wealth and power. It lulls the moderately well off into a complacent sense that all is well with economic life. By artificially increasing the pressure on the less well-off and the poor, it deepens their economic dependency. In each of these ways it stimulates an unnecessarily high level of economic activity and the ecological damage which results. Thus interest is opposed for the very reason it was opposed by the medieval church – because it harms life.[5]

On the basis of what has been said in his earlier chapters it is hard to see how Gorringe could have come to any other conclusion; and on the basis of what has been said in the earlier chapters of this book it is hard not to agree. The power of money, and in particular the right of those who have money to use it to make more money, and with less and less restraint, makes the observation that the institutions of usury 'harm' life a dramatic understatement: we now know, and see the evidence all around us, that they *destroy* life.

The clarity of the tradition

It is also clear that those who would mount a defence of usury, let alone the other contemporary means of making money out of money, have a formidable task of explanation in relation to the huge weight of Christian tradition ranged against the practice. Indeed it is on the basis of a far smaller quantity of material drawn from that very same tradition that other areas of ethical debate have been deemed beyond discussion or revision. In his detailed history of early Christian thinking on the subject of wealth, Justo González is unable to find a single source for a positive attitude to usury, meaning not exorbitant rates but any loan at interest (with the possible exception of Clement of Alexandria, and even there the doubt rests on a disputed interpretation of a single text which suggests that the ban on usury might only apply to loans to other believers). Otherwise,

> Christian writers throughout the first four centuries are practically unanimous in their rejection of usury as well as of any loan on interest, and for this they draw both on Old Testament law and on the Greco-Roman tradition that held usury in contempt, even though a moderate rate of interest was legal according to civil law.[6]

So in holding to this view, early Christians were following not merely the clear statements of Old Testament law condemning the practice – which the New Testament church, while not discussing the topic specifically, clearly assumes – but the general view derived from Hellenistic culture. Plutarch, like many before him, wrote 'Against running into debt or taking up money in usury', opposing it on the grounds that the borrower is in the power of the lender, and that such borrowing is in any case (he assumes) not for the meeting of genuine need but for luxuries;[7] in any case, moneylending is unnatural because, in words that could well sum up some of our earlier reflections on the character of money, 'nothing arises out of nothing; for with these men interest arises out of that which has as yet no being or existence.'[8] This last point echoes Aristotle's comment, making full play with the significance of the Greek for interest, *tokos*, which is also the word for 'offspring':

> The most hated sort [of wealth-getting], and with good reason, is usury, which makes a gain out of money itself, and not from the natural object of it. For money was intended to be used in exchange, but not to increase at interest. And this term interest [*tokos*], which means the birth of money from money, is applied to the breeding of money because the offspring resembles the parent. Wherefore of all the methods of getting wealth this is the most unnatural.[9]

Roman law permitted the lending of money at interest, at a maximum rate of one per cent simple interest per month; but the practice was still disapproved of by moralists and philosophers, so that Cicero, for example, classed moneylending with tax-gathering as a sordid occupation on the grounds that it inevitably created ill will; naturally enough, therefore, he was horrified when he encountered an interest rate as high as 48 per cent.[10]

For the early Christian Church to have supported the lending of money at interest would have involved a marked break with the surrounding culture, and there is no evidence that such a break was ever contemplated. That is hardly surprising given the strong biblical injunctions against it. The tradition of opposition continued: usury was expressly forbidden to clergy by the Councils of Arles (314) and Nicaea (325), the ban being extended to laity by the first Council of Carthage (348) and the Council of Aix (789). There was a formal condemnation of the practice at the Third Lateran Council (1179) and the Second Council of Lyons (1274). The reformers Luther and Zwingli strenuously maintained the tradition, and even though Calvin proposed some acceptance of the practice, it was under strictly limited conditions; the ban on usury was for the protection of the poor, and usurers who are idle and simply profit from the labours of others were to be condemned. Although Calvin has come to be remembered more for his admitting of usury than for the qualifications with which he accepted it (Preston regards him as 'more far-seeing' than the other reformers[11]), it is clear that acceptance of moneylending came in only with great hesitation and reluctance. Given the strength and unanimity of the tradition that is hardly surprising.[12]

Some reasons for doubt

Given the widespread acceptance of credit and debt today, there are of course many who would argue that this tradition, for all its weight, cannot be decisive for the Church in present-day circumstances; and in fairness it is important to enter some words of caution about it. Our sources may exhibit a high degree of unanimity up to the time of the Reformation (after which the issue of debt makes far fewer appearances until the present period), but that still leaves the question of what we are to gather from these sources about the *actual practice* of Church members. The presence of a tradition of theology and even of developing legislation against lending money at interest may tell us that those responsible for theology and the developing canons of the Church disapproved of the practice; but that *may* in effect suggest that the practice was in fact quite widespread. Our sources are theologians and the decrees of Church councils, but these are chiefly the products of bishops – what was the actual practice of lay Christians?

If clergy in particular were forbidden to engage in usury, does this not suggest that some in fact had done so? If this was later extended to laity, and then centuries later the condemnation had to be repeated, does not this also suggest that the Church in fact included among its wealthier members a number who were lending money at interest? And (the argument would run) if the tradition against usury was in fact apparently honoured more in the breach than in the observance, does not that mean that the approval of moneylending that has accelerated in the last three centuries represents a proper concession to the inevitable, and a progressive end to the hypocrisy of maintaining in theory what cannot be held to in practice? And who can really value the *integrity* of this tradition when we know that it led to the decree of the Fourth Lateran Council (1215) to allow only Jews to lend money at interest, something that cast a long and sinister shadow over Jewish–Christian relations for centuries to come. If a principle is only maintained at the cost of such a series of double standards, should we not be glad that things have developed in a more honest and realistic direction?

Whether the developments that have led to our present enthusiastic approach to borrowing and lending should properly be described as a growth in honesty and realism we shall need to consider, not least in the light of all that previous chapters have shown us of the severe consequences of the way in which capitalism is currently practised; but as Stephen Lea's researches show that in general people are more likely to approve of debt if they themselves are in it,[13] we have to accept that the increasing approval of usury followed its increasing practice, rather than the other way round.

Certainly what Max Weber and R. H. Tawney describe[14] is the progressive acceptance of that development; but we need to be clear that that is an example of the growing autonomy of all kinds of reason, in this case the increasing separation of religious considerations from economic and political ones. The emergence – we may say with Bonhoeffer, the coming of age – of *homo oeconomicus*, the autonomous regulator of social norms and economic practice without any 'religious *a priori*', is very much part of the challenge to develop an answer to the question, 'Who is Jesus Christ for us today?' For nowadays there would be widespread sympathy within Christian circles for the view that a ban on the lending of money at interest is totally out of the question, and any debate there is turns on the question of whether any regulation of moneylending is either desirable or possible. Not many who regard themselves as Christian believers take the view that religious belief can be decisive in the management of the economy; mostly the plea is for 'realism', and it is not a realism that has the reality of God much in mind.

In the face of the progressive abandonment of any opposition to the lending of money at interest it is not surprising that there has been a search by some with theologically troubled consciences for historical or theological means of distancing present-day lenders and investors from the troublesome scruples of the past. For example, there would now be widespread accept-ance that the ban on lending money at interest arose in a context in which the assumption was that any debt would arise from need and that therefore the charging of any interest would be exploitation. On that basis it seems quite reasonable to say that in the modern economy, where debt is for production or con-sumption, it is therefore perfectly admissible that the person providing the capital, and therefore foregoing the use of it, should gain some profit as a result.[15] This distinction, between lending for need and lending for consumption, survives in Jewish and Islamic communities today, where charging interest is not allowed if the loan is to meet a person's need.

Not only do such doubts exist about the biblical and traditional legislation for the *control* of lending and the charging of interest; similar doubts are frequently raised about the relevance of the biblical provisions of the *remedying* of debt, chiefly the jubilee and sabbatical year traditions. The provision for a general remission or suspension of debt and release of debt slaves every seven years and a restoration of land to its original owners every fifty years is the subject of a good deal of scholarly discussion.[16] Certainly it was not intended to discourage people from lending to those in need for, as Blount remarks,

> It is quite wrong . . . to argue that legislation on debt remission and the banning of interest is designed to dis-courage lenders from lending; any tendency in that direction through 'market forces' is expressly counteracted and lending is positively encouraged as a good work.[17]

Deuteronomy 15:9 is quite clear on the point: 'Be careful that you do not entertain a mean thought, thinking, "The seventh year, the year of remission, is near," and therefore view your needy neighbour with hostility and give nothing; your neighbour might cry to the Lord against you, and you would incur guilt.'

Again, however, a text such as this, while encouragingly firm in its demand for compassion, raises the same disturbing question we encountered in considering all the canons against usury developed by the early Christian councils: does not this command in fact bear witness to what must have been a serious practical difficulty about the jubilee legislation for debt remission? Again, there is much scholarly debate about whether the jubilee in fact happened as it was commanded; whether the year in which it was to happen was the forty-ninth or the fiftieth; whether there could possibly have been, in an agrarian society, a universal fallow year; and whether the release of slaves was a national event or was due to each slave after six years' service.[18] Certainly the practicalities of observing a jubilee are complex, even within the different setting of early Palestine, and we are not told explicitly that it was regularly observed; the only event of the kind is described in Nehemiah 5, and while the evils of indebtedness and usury are described there, there is no appeal to the legislation requiring a regular jubilee. So although it is always dangerous to argue from silence, in this case to the conclusion that the jubilee never happened, we may properly wonder whether it was enacted as a regular event over any prolonged period.

But that does not allow us to dismiss the jubilee tradition as purely visionary and utopian, not intended to be made a practical reality. For the wealth of practical regulations and the precautions against attempts to circumvent them suggest that there is more here than mere 'vision'. The Sabbath and jubilee laws were also, for all their difficulty, 'an evolving attempt to deal with a matter of justice in the community at a practical level and in a way that belongs to the embedded economy of the time in its mixing of religious, social and economic concerns.'[19]

But it is also right to stress the point, as Blount does, that the biblical 'embedded economy' – that is, one in which transactions we call economic are embedded in ties of kinship and community – is totally different from the market economy of modern times, and the legislative interventions contained in the Bible would not serve the same purpose or have the same effect in a modern setting as they would have had originally. In considering the economy of the Hebrew and Jewish community we are considering a predominantly rural one in which a close-knit social fabric operated to make the transactions of borrowing and lending part of what sustained the life of the community and enabled the poor to survive. The protection of the needy and the maintenance of the life of the clan and the wider community was inseparable from the way in which trade and agriculture were organised. In such a context, clearly, the exploitation of the destitute was to be condemned, and what is more steps were to be taken regularly to prevent processes of oppression taking hold.

For economies in the ancient world were governed by the unquestioned acceptance of what Malina calls, writing of the New Testament period in particular, 'the perception of limited good', an understanding of the world that conditioned most of the rules of behaviour.

> The majority of the people of the time lived in villages or in artisan quarters of the preindustrial city. For this majority (and perhaps the minority élite as well), the main perception in life was that all goods are limited. This perception lies behind the behavior considered necessary for an adequate human existence.[20]

In such a world one person's increase of prosperity was another person's decrease; there was no idea of a prospect of a general increase of wealth that was not at somebody's expense, and therefore the primary concern of each person was to maintain in quantity and good order the inheritance of their clan or family. Borrowing could only be a reflection of hard times; the charging of interest could only be exploitative; and the return of lands, the remission of debts and the freeing of slaves were the necessary provisions of a society determined to maintain the just order of community life which accorded with God's intention.

As part of the commitment of the Jewish people to living out the justice of God, that also meant that the terms of loans and the methods for their recovery had to be controlled: invasion of a person's home to take what was pledged for a loan was forbidden (Deuteronomy 24:10 ff); and what was taken in pledge must not be something, such as a millstone, which would be the borrower's only means of livelihood (Deuteronomy 24:6), or their essential protection against the night cold (Exodus 22:25–6). Transgression against such controls on the activities of lenders would contribute to the destruction of the life of the community and would prevent a borrower in hard times ever being restored to an adequate standard of living.

These major differences between the politics and economy of biblical times and those of our own have all been pointed to in support of the contention that the control of debt and usury as it was exercised then cannot be applied in modern times. The claim is made that the world has greatly and irrevocably changed. Perhaps we could allow that the wisdom of our forebears may have been appropriate to their very different world (though even there the laws were enforced with difficulty and with patchy success), but we now live in a different world, the argument would run, one where we have known massive increases in wealth overall, where value has been added to products and services without being extracted from others, and where there-fore all have benefited by the ingenuity with which particular people have invested in the development of new products and services to everyone's advantage. None of that would be possible, the argument continues, if we made the attempt to reinstate the rules of an agrarian economy. Above all, we cannot seriously propose that mere conservation of a person's heritage should be the limit of their ambition, rather than its improvement. Is it not the case that even the world's poorest desire those things which have only been made possible by the development of a capitalist, technologically based, economy?

In these doubts about the relevance of the biblical control on lending, and remedies for indebtedness, there is both truth and self-deception. It is true that we inhabit a totally different world, and that part of that difference arises precisely from the effects of several centuries of capitalist economic development. Those changes cannot be undone, and render it foolish to suppose that we could simply revert from where we are to where they were. We cannot again become, certainly not quickly and almost cer-tainly ever, a rural, local economy.

But there is also profound self-deception in the idealisation of our present circumstances. There may indeed be a record of wealth creation that has given great benefit to many and indeed holds out the promise, perhaps, of even more; but to suggest that wealth is generally being created at nobody's expense is just to ignore the huge amount of evidence, a small part of which is contained in Chapters 3 and 5, that the cost to the world's most vulnerable of our present methods of 'wealth creation' is enormous; at the very least one must say that while there may be *some* wealth creation that is not at someone's expense, there is a great deal that is. We do well to reflect also that the provisions designed to prevent indebtedness getting out of hand derived a large part of their force from deeply etched folk memory about what happens when it does: in listening to the Old Testament we are hearing the voices of those who recalled the slavery, the suffering and the social unrest which debt had occasioned. If we find the rules dated, the experience is not; it becomes more and more current with the passing of the years.

More than that: the fact that during the centuries of industrialisation developments have been enabled that have taken the economy out of its rural roots and into a global context does not mean that the process can simply be continued, and at the ever-increasing speed we observe, forever into the future. It may be true that the economy of biblical times was based in villages where the most that any family could expect was to conserve what it had and so survive. The truth may also be that centuries of capitalist and technological development have simply brought us to the point where we all inhabit a village again – a global one. And this village may be one in which we can give attention to the conservation of what our one human family has been given, in such matters as the diversity of species, the variety of the world's beauty, and even the very resources we need for our survival. Maybe we cannot return at a stroke to the arena in which that ancient wisdom evolved; but maybe the wisdom is returning to offer us the way forward we need.

Jubilee from Nazareth

Eleazar was a smallholder who got a miserable living from his land. A few years ago we had one bad harvest after another over a period. Eleazar had to eat his seed grain in order to avoid starvation. New seed was dear because of the general scarcity of grain. Anyone who had any grain left did well, but the poor fared worse than ever. Eleazar got into debt. He couldn't pay it back. What was he to do? Was he to sell his children on the slave market in Tyre, as others had? Never. Was he to sell himself and his family to a richer Jew, to ensure his freedom at most after seven years? Should he wait until his creditors took him before the judge to have him imprisoned for debt? And then watch his wife going downhill? Eleazar was a proud man. He rebelled against the threat of disaster. He and his family vanished into the hills.[21]

We have not so far mentioned a further reason that causes many

Christian believers to doubt the relevance of the Old Testament
injunctions about lending and borrowing to a response to indebtedness: the absence of any systematic instruction from the New
Testament about how such matters were to be handled within
the Christian community, let alone in the relations of Christians
to the world around them. For there is a rather widespread
scepticism about the application of the Jewish tradition in the
modern world on the part of those who in a popular understanding of the nature of Christianity see it as having
'transcended' its roots in the history of Israel and the Jewish
people. (There is a terrible irony here in the use of such arguments by a Church which thought usury so wrong that only
Jews should practise it.)

This is not the place to engage in a detailed debate about the
relationship of early Christianity to its Jewish inheritance; for
the most part the early Church presupposed its own essential
Jewishness, and as we have seen there is every evidence that the
conviction was maintained for centuries that lending money at
interest was wrong. What needs to be noticed here is the extent
to which the world of the New Testament in fact presupposes
the existence of a widespread problem of indebtedness. Theissen's
imaginative reconstruction of the story of Jesus, from which is
taken the account of an incident in Nazareth quoted above,
certainly suggests that indebtedness figured among the essential
ingredients of the social scene into which Christ came and from
which Christianity emerged.

Theissen here portrays the possibility that Jewish, as against
Gentile, slavery was seen as relatively privileged, certainly to the
extent that the law of release prevailed; he makes the point that
those texts such as 'You shall not get out of [prison] until you
have paid the last penny' (Matthew 5:26) and the parable of
the large and small debts (Matthew 18:23–35) are really only
comprehensible if we assume an audience for Jesus' teaching well
acquainted with the hopeless situation in which debtors often
found themselves.[22] Luke's account of the opening of Jesus' ministry in the synagogue at Nazareth, the sounding of the call to
jubilee, recaptures a body of biblical teaching rooted in the
experience of indebtedness, and was remembered by an audience
who themselves knew it well.

The Spirit of the Lord is upon me, because he has anointed

me to bring good news to the poor. He has sent me to
proclaim release to the captives and recovery of sight to the
blind, to let the oppressed go free, to proclaim the year of
the Lord's favour.

(Luke 4:18–19)

This was the scripture that Jesus declared to have been fulfilled
that day in the presence of his hearers (Luke 4:21). The Jubilee
sounded from Nazareth.

This was a world in which peasants living mainly in villages
found many ways into debt and few ways out of it.

When peasant producers under pressure for taxes did not
have enough grain and oil to feed their families until the
next harvest after rendering both to Caesar's agents and to
God's, their only alternative would have been to borrow.
But the limited resources of fellow villagers and of neigh-
bouring villages would have been quickly exhausted.
Hence, hungry peasants would have been forced to seek
loans from those who controlled larger stores of grain, oil,
or money.[23]

This is the picture, as described by Richard Horsley in his
Sociology and the Jesus Movement, that is also depicted in Jesus'
illustrations from the daily life of his predominantly peasant
audience. What is more, the evidence of Josephus' description
of the setting on fire by insurgents of the debt archives in
Jerusalem (*Jewish War* 2:427) suggests that the authorities in Jerusalem who were responsible for the levying of both Roman
tribute and temple tax were the same as those who held the debt
records. 'That is, those who provided and controlled credit were
the very rulers of the system that placed the difficult economic
demands in the first place.'[24]

The relationship between lenders and borrowers was indeed
complex, and the causes of indebtedness likewise. In his
extremely detailed assessment of the economic situation in Jesus'
time, Douglas Oakman describes a web of lending and borrowing
which is indeed tangled, but which at the same time bears
an uncomfortable resemblance to the dynamics of indebtedness
evolving in our own society and in relationships between debtor
and creditor nations. He considers many possible sources of
pressure to borrow, including poor harvests, and pressure from

increased population requiring smallholders to borrow in order to purchase more land. In fact, however, there is not a great deal of evidence of famine in the time of Jesus, nor do we have much evidence of deals to acquire more land with borrowed money. In the end Oakman makes a persuasive case, backed with parallels from other parts of the Roman empire, that while on the one hand much additional revenue was flowing into the city from trade, giving rise to a surplus of money there, at the same time excessive demands were being made on the peasantry. 'Not only was wealth from trade available to the urban aristocracy to loan, and not only did they need to invest it, but their demands for tithes and tributes, combined with the demands of the Roman state, were forcing the peasantry to borrow.'[25] So the pressure that led to the need to borrow came from many of those very groups that were happy to lend. In reading such accounts one is easily reminded of the legacy of the decade of the petro-dollar, where the need to lend and the demand for large payments often came from the same direction.

It is not difficult to see how Jesus' teaching would have been understood in a world in which the life of a people under occupation, and with a quisling monarchy determined to extract the best it could from the situation, would create an environment in which taxes, tributes and rents would progressively result in the impoverishment of more and more of the rural population and the poor's reduction to a position close to slavery. In such circumstances people borrowed from each other to survive in any way they could, and the mercilessness contained in the system would infect all social relationships.

Any change in this situation must involve, as John Howard Yoder describes it, the transformation of relationships, the enactment of jubilee, at every level; there can be no jubilee for those who do not participate in it in relation to their fellow-citizens.[26] Oakman makes the same point, pointing out also the contrasting situation portrayed in Luke 7:41-3, where two debtors, one owing ten times the debt of the other, are both released from their debts when they are unable to pay. Jesus, speaking in the house of Simon the Pharisee, asks which would love the creditor more, and uses the obvious answer to compare the response of the woman who had anointed him with that of Simon himself. For the remission of debt to function as so powerful and clear a means of teaching it is certain that the dire consequences of debt must have been a prevalent experience, and there are good grounds for seeing in that the reason why the jubilee of debt remission came to be so prominent an image of the liberation brought by Jesus.

The fact that indebtedness and remission of debt function as a means of teaching about all social relationships, and in turn about the relationship between humanity and God, must not allow us to suppose that its material and financial reference becomes somehow dispensable. We do not have to accept our earlier quotation from Nietzsche to the effect that the buyer–seller relationship is the origin of all moral discourse to accept, nevertheless, that owing money or property remain very powerful experiences which intrude themselves into the other obligations we 'owe'. The importance of this is evident immediately we come to look at one of the central occasions of the use of the language of indebtedness, namely the petition for forgiveness in the Lord's Prayer. The meaning is transformed if the financial roots of the language are taken with full seriousness.

So C. F. Evans, for example, gives a most sensitive account of the experience of indebtedness and release as a model for relationships with God; but because like many he does not consider the material basis of the experience to be particularly significant he portrays the language of the remission of debt entirely as metaphor, and, in relation to other available metaphors, not a particularly important one in the total witness of the New Testament.[27] In many expositions, the material and financial importance of the language of indebtedness is lost in a process of 'spiritualisation' which, profound as it is, has given rise to a whole tradition of interpretation, and with this an obscuring of the radical transformation for which the prayer asks.

Oakman, on the other hand, regards the petition as one for 'release from the earthly shackles of indebtedness. The problem of debt, oppressing the people of Palestine and controlling their lives, is so vast that only God's power can effectively remove it.'[28] Significantly, even the Lucan version of the prayer, which removes mention of debt from the request to God for forgiveness, retains it in the condition of the prayer, 'as we forgive those who are indebted to us', and in both the verb used is that of debt remission.

What is even more important to our perception of the power

of the material aspect of indebtedness, however, is the link that Oakman makes with the previous petition for our daily bread:

Indebtedness threatens the availability of daily bread. Conversely, the petition for daily bread is at the same time a petition for a social order that will supply such basic human needs in a regular and consistent manner. Thus, the succeeding petition for forgiveness can be seen to address in another way this same concern: indebtedness disrupts the ability of a social order to supply daily bread. God is petitioned to remove the oppressive power of debt in people's lives.[29]

The marginalised for whom Jesus made such a consistent option included many of those forced into prostitution, tax collection or other occupations separated from the rural economy; and in many cases this enforced separation, and therefore their becoming 'sinners', will have arisen, we may well surmise, from their experience of becoming victims of impoverishment by debt. So they would understand well enough just how dramatic would be the transformation God was able to effect for those who had co-operated in God's jubilee on earth. 'Bread and debt were quite simply the two most immediate problems facing the Galilean peasant, day labourer and non-élite urbanite. Alleviation of these two anxieties would be the most obvious benefits of God's reign.'[30]

The jubilee economy

We are seeing already that the claim that the Old Testament legislation for the control of borrowing and lending was in some way superseded by a New Testament that had little concern for such matters is profoundly myopic. True, the movement inaugurated by Jesus and carried on by the early Church had no expectation that it would have civic authority or be able to exercise legislative responsibility for the national economy. But the movement arose in a context of economic distortion that included a dominant debt economy which was having dire consequences. Jesus' teaching not only drew many of its illustrations from that dislocated economic life but attracted a following of people among whom a conspicuous group were those who knew very well at first hand the kind of social situation he was describing. As has been owned many times, the translation of Jesus' proclamation of remission from his own society into one as complex and different as our own, let alone into the international economic order, is an undertaking of huge difficulty; but to recognise that is by no means to agree that an economy free of domination by credit and debt is a part of an Old Testament understanding of society for which the New Testament has no place.

There is a further and even more compelling reason for taking the New Testament seriously in a consideration of these issues. It is that it offers an account not simply of what Jesus did and said, but also of the beginnings of the community to which his movement gave rise, the Church. And it is absolutely clear that from the beginning it was understood that the Church was to have a certain economic character, and that belonging to it would involve financial consequences for the disciples. For some the consequence would be the lifting of the burden of poverty and the relief which came from participation in a common life – a life which, even if it did not produce riches or what *we* should call financial security, nevertheless offered the assurance of belonging to an economic community.

We hear the positive side of this in Acts 2:44 ff, 'All who believed were together and had all things in common; they would sell their possessions and goods and distribute the proceeds to all, as any had need'. But in the story of Ananias' and Sapphira's deception we also hear that the financial demands of discipleship were such that some would seek to evade them:

> 'Ananias,' Peter asked, 'why has Satan filled your heart to lie to the Holy Spirit and to keep back part of the proceeds of the land? While it remained unsold, did it not remain your own? And after it was sold, were not the proceeds at your disposal? How is it that you have contrived this deed in your heart? You did not lie to us but to God.'
>
> (Acts 5:3–4)

From their ensuing death we certainly learn that the earliest Christian community required that people address the issue of money with great seriousness; this is confirmed by the warnings in the pastoral epistles. There is an uncomfortable contrast

between our contemporary requirements for pastoral office that
a person shall not be in debt and the New Testament requirement
that a bishop should not be a lover of money (1 Timothy 3:3):
ostentatious wealth was evidently considered more of a bar to
pastoral leadership than poverty.[31] The same applied to deacons
(1 Timothy 3:8); and the warnings 'Keep your lives free from
the love of money' (Hebrews 13:5) and 'People will be . . . lovers
of money' (2 Timothy 3:2) are encapsulated in an aphorism
which we may assume was the fruit of hard experience, that 'the
love of money is the root of all kinds of evil' (1 Timothy 6:10).

But if there were any doubt that Jesus' ministry had left behind
a gospel in which the meaning of money was not merely a key
implication of faith but was of the very character of faith, this
doubt would have to be dispelled by the remarkable interweaving
of the economic with the spiritual in the matter of the collection
Paul makes for the Church in Jerusalem (2 Corinthians 8—9).
In their account of *Meaning and Truth in 2 Corinthians*, Frances
Young and David Ford have no qualms about describing Paul's
message as having to do with a divine 'economy',[31] and relating
it directly to the experiences of debt, slavery, inheritance and
other aspects of the actual economic experience of his hearers.
God's economy is superabundant, a point of particular importance in the light of Malina's point, mentioned already, that the
economy of the time would have been one of 'limited good'.

But this superabundance which characterises God's economy
is not to lead, in the manner of capitalist superabundance, to
acquisitiveness, but to an overflowing generosity, in which
Christians reflect in their own life 'the generous act of our Lord
Jesus Christ, [who] though he was rich for our sake became
poor, so that by his poverty you might become rich' (2 Corinthians 8:9). This should issue in a concern for the sharing of
burdens, not to produce 'relief for others and pressure on you,
but . . . a fair balance between your present abundance and their
need, so that their abundance may be for your need, in order
that there may be a balance' (8:13 ff). The Corinthians are to
be inspired by the Macedonian churches who have manifested,
even in the midst of their own destitution, the kind of generosity
he seeks. Again the mixture of material and spiritual resources
so characteristic of these two chapters runs through the passage
(8:1 ff):

We want you to know, brothers and sisters, about the grace of God that has been granted to the Churches of Macedonia, for during a severe ordeal of affliction, their abundant joy and their extreme poverty have overflowed in a wealth of generosity on their part.

The divine economy is not merely superabundant: it is one in which generosity yields more generosity in turn. Drawing on the lessons of a rural economy, Paul is nevertheless able to encourage his hearers with the message of unlimited good, once again material and spiritual, bound inseparably together (9:6–10):

The one who sows sparingly will also reap sparingly, and the one who sows bountifully will also reap bountifully. Each of you must give as you have made up your mind, not reluctantly or under compulsion, for God loves a cheerful giver. And God is able to provide you with every blessing in abundance, so that by always having enough of everything, you may share abundantly in every good work. As it is written, 'He scatters abroad, he gives to the poor; his righteousness endures for ever.' He who supplies seed to the sower and bread for food will supply and multiply your seed for sowing and increase the harvest of your righteousness.

It is of course possible to present this account as simply the magnificent, though manipulative, rhetoric of Paul, 'the apostle as fund-raiser', as Graham Shaw does in his account of the role of manipulation of all kinds in the exercise of authority in the New Testament period, drawing attention to Paul's appeal to competitive instincts in 'quite shamelessly playing off one congregation to another'.[32] Without wishing to debate here Shaw's highly suspicious interpretation, his account makes one thing quite clear: if Paul was using techniques that worked, they worked because they related to the actual experience of his hearers. The language was able to perform its task because it spoke to a community that knew both the poverty of a debt economy and the superabundant outcomes of the new economy that the Church practised. The blessings of every kind were precisely not the ones the old economy offered at the expense of others, but the spiritual and material communion that came

to those who sought to live out in the body of Christ the jubilee
that he had declared.

The appeal to the Corinthian church to be generous in the
face of the need of the Jerusalem community was also and
inseparably an appeal to the generosity they had experienced in
their common life. This was specifically not a demand to repay
a debt, but to understand the meaning and nature of a gift. It
accords with, and is simply the economic expression of, the
central thrust of Paul's theology, as expressed elsewhere in
Romans and Galatians: the divine strategy is not to do with
earnings, repayments, debt-collectors, and the like, but the out-
pouring of a generosity that hopes for generosity as a result. It
is a new kind of obligation, grounded in the experience of
freedom rather than the powerlessness of poverty to resist
demand. Because of their experience, and ours, of a world of
credit and debt, the divine economy – one in which, as C. K.
Barrett puts it, 'there is no conflict between the theology of
freedom and the ethics of obligation'[33] – will always appear as
paradox. What is certain is that, as for the early Church, any
resolution has to have effect in the economy of our life together.

Wisdom rediscovered; faith required

When it comes to the management of resources in society, we
are heirs to an ancient and demanding wisdom. It comes from
a world vastly different from our own, which we have been
taught to consider primitive and many of whose privations we
are mightily glad to have transcended. We have learned to attribute much of that improvement in our material standard of living
to the ingenuity with which resources have been invested and
human drive and ambition harnessed to create prosperity of a
kind that our forebears could never have envisaged even in
their wildest dreams. The prosperous élites of ancient societies,
flaunting their wealth, are still there; but they have been joined
in our generation by a mass culture of consumption in which
possibilities of choice and enjoyment present themselves very
widely. We have seen new worlds accessed by people who in
earlier generations could never have aspired to them.

It is not hard in such circumstances to turn our eyes away

from those who are not – or, as we may try to hope, not yet – beneficiaries of such progress. And when our eyes are drawn to them we tend to see in them not so much an indictment of the means of progress we have used, or even a qualification of the virtues we ascribe to these, but only a reason to double our stake and press on. What has worked for the world's prosperous societies will surely come to work for its less prosperous ones; and if it is true (as we uncomfortably have to admit it is) that even in prosperous societies there are those who are not yet prospering, that may well be their fault . . . or, if it is their misfortune, how can the rest of us be responsible for that? Add to that the collapse of alternative political and economic ideologies, and how can we fail to see that the only way forward must be to proceed with, and to accelerate, the processes of investment and commercial lending that have brought us at least this far?

We avert our attention from the evidence that it is those very processes which have so fed upon themselves that acceleration is built into them, and that arresting them appears beyond the bounds of possibility even if we could bring ourselves to try. There has seemed on that basis to be an overwhelming case for consigning the arrangements made by our forebears to history. To those who in any way seek to reinstate aspects of them we attribute simply a nostalgic longing for the past, judging them to be people whom we need not respect because they themselves are happy to enjoy the fruits that have come from the techno-logical and economic ingenuity of those recent centuries when borrowing and lending came of age, rescued from those who would protect and control them.

Yet we have seen that it is precisely the arguments for the irrelevance of our inherited economic wisdom that are now revealed as arrogance in the face of the desperate plight of the world's poor and the threat to the world's resources. We have, as has been said, grown out of our village life, only to find that the global village has enclosed us again. We have supposed that we could all be winners in a process of wealth creation that would produce gains for all and losses for none, only to find not only an ever-increasing army of losers, but that loss is quite evidently threatening us all. The evidence of the mountain of debt and the world in debt brings us curiously closer to the environment which generated the ancient wisdom about the dangers of money's power and attractiveness, its essential barrenness and infertility belied by the profits that can be made with it – profits which are just more money like that from which they were made.

In the face of all the interests that profit from its forgetting the reassertion of that wisdom is a formidable task, involving new thinking not just about the control of credit and debt but, as we have seen, the reform of those institutions of governance that progressively make nonsense of many of our social and political institutions by subjugating them to the power of money. It is a task of political will, courage and much economic skill, a skill that is often lacking because neither the political will nor the courage is present. But that is not all that is involved.

A verdict of irrelevance passed on the social and economic wisdom of the past turns quickly into a similar verdict of irrelevance on the experience of Jesus' first hearers; and therefore, much as this would be denied, upon the good news they found in his life and his words. What other verdict is one pronouncing if one accepts the separation of Jesus' words from the social experience to which they were addressed? We suppose that the materiality of his illustrations and the hard facts of his encounters on the one hand with the marginalised and on the other with the centres of economic, social and religious power are some mere scenery, a backdrop to the 'real' story, changeable at will and dispensable once you have turned from the actual illustration to the 'teaching' it contains.

Yet this disembodied 'teaching', this mere spirituality without materiality, described in terms of scenes from life which we can glance at before we pass on, leaves us with little to connect us to the movement of which Jesus was the creator. Separate him from his community and from the ancient economic and social wisdom that both he and his first hearers honoured, whose neglect was the subject of his sternest warnings, and we are left with an ancient set of inaccessible metaphors. To re-establish such wisdom in terms that can begin to grapple with the issues of our time and arrest its money-driven determination to press on is a task not just of political manipulation but above all, if political change is to happen, of personal conversion also.

The movement Jesus occasioned did in fact, even if not always and not always successfully, enable its members to trust less in money and the security it claims to offer and to engage with one another in ways which transcended the credit and debt relationships that they had found so damaging to their lives and to their society. If the experience of writing this book is anything to go by, finding the means, and even describing the issues, is hard precisely because it brings one face to face with the social and personal consequences that serious discipleship involves. When we speak of the world of unrestrained credit and debt we do indeed find ourselves face to face with Bonhoeffer's question, 'Who is Jesus Christ for us today?' It is a faith question, refined sharply by the contrast we have made between the divine and human economies: asking who Christ is means asking who *we* are *economically*: debtor? creditor? disciple seeking a community of jubilee? So too the economy obliges us to ask who is the 'us' we mean when speak of 'Jesus Christ for *us* today': with whom do we locate ourselves in a world of injustice – with those who have or those who have not? And we are asked too, whose 'today' have we in mind – the today of those who have control of the economy and who decide its timetable, or of those who juggle their debts from one collector to the next in order to make it to the end of the week because they have no escape from debt?

So it turns out that among the casualties of this forgetting of an ancient wisdom about the power of money and the need to control its lending is also the substance of faith, a faith that always expects spiritual truth, the shape and meaning of human life, the largest questions of our living and dying, to be clothed in flesh, eaten in food, paid for with real resources. We are back again with Bonhoeffer's two criteria against which the truth of any answer to the question 'Who is Jesus Christ for us today?' must be measured: it must speak to the actual, material, secular, day-to-day experience of people, and it must address them at their point of strength and not just when they experience themselves as weak.

So the ancient wisdom about money, not at all irrelevant but among the things we urgently need for the humanising of the world economy, turns out to bring with it access to an ancient faith as well. That is something we also urgently require if we would dare to engage with such desperately intractable economic realities. Speaking of Jesus Christ for us today may turn out not just to meet the perplexity of a post-Christian culture still carrying a vocabulary, a narrative and a practice of worship which it cannot connect with the largest questions of its life. It may also empower us for the repentance and renewal that themselves need liberating from the disembodied world of mere religion into engagement with some of the greatest challenges facing humankind, so as to have once again what the gospel had when first it appeared in its own debt-laden world: a real connection to reality, what significantly we now call 'cash value'.

Captured in John Nicholson's recent set of meditations on the Lord's Prayer is not only the intimate connection made by Oakman between liberation from debt and the possibility of daily bread for all, but the consequences in living and believing for those who seek them:

> Prompt us to the daily dying
> which frees the gift of bread for all;
> And as we roll back the stones
> we used to burden others,
> May we come to see that we too
> are rising in your love.[34]

The economy of freedom

'You seem to regard debt as always a bad thing.' That comment, in a conversation about the progress of this book, represented a real challenge to my exploration. For the remorseless parading of the explosion of credit and debt in our own society and the devastating results of a world economy built on a mountain of debt can only leave the impression that lending and borrowing are all about power, that indebtedness can only disable, that no good can come out of it. The mind and heart rebel against such an idea, and rejoice to acknowledge that there are debts one can accrue in one's life about which one is glad, things one has received that one cannot imagine one's life without and that one feels bound to recognise even if – perhaps especially if – one can never repay them. But these debts, you may reply, are not financial ones, not the ones this book is looking at.

Owing and giving

There is a man – I do not know his name – whom I met briefly in the corrugated iron hut where a friend of his lived on the outskirts of Bulawayo. He was part of a congregation gathered for a eucharist while I was visiting. His legs had had to be amputated and he sat through the service in an old wheelchair. At the end of the service there was some conversation in Ndebele which I did not understand, and they took up a collection. The man said something and it was explained to me that he was saying he only had three cents to put in. Then they came and gave me the money. My interpreter said, 'They are saying that as you will have been away from your children for a long time, when you get home you should buy them some sweets with this money.'

It was a financial transaction: three cents is a sum of money, in the world of money a negligible sum. In my world, and I believe also in the world of Jesus who saw a widow put such small coins in the treasury, it was a vast sum, beyond counting, let alone repayment, a sum too small to translate into English currency and yet more than all the gold in Fort Knox could purchase. Yet, you may say, this was not a loan but a gift. Nobody expects repayment of it; it constitutes no debt. Is that so? Does not receiving such a gift – indeed a gift of money – create a debt? Do I owe nothing to this man who gave me his three cents? Am I free to say 'thank you' and walk away unchanged? Am I not in some sense *obliged* by what has happened? And is not this obligation, this debt, profoundly enriching? Is a human life conceivable that is not in some sense constituted by such debts that are beyond repayment? And if the debt cannot be repaid, is there not some response that *is due*, some recognition that *is owed*?

Yet one's mind rebels against the suggestion that between the receiving and the responding somebody is being *paid back* for something. What might a person do who has received such a gift as I was given? Or perhaps we might ask, what might such a person *become* as a result? Maybe there would happen some deep changes in attitude: maybe a modification of some of the condescension that pervades the mindset of those who have and 'help' those who have not. Maybe some melting of the receiver's own meanness, a disturbing of some latent remaining racism. Maybe a decision to become more involved in a campaign to change the poverty-making structures of international trade so that, for example, this man's friend could have something a bit more comfortable to live in than a leaking corrugated iron hut. Maybe a determination to share the story with others, so that they too could reflect on it. Maybe a warmer reverence for a eucharistic celebration grown cold in the polite and well-ordered circumstances of churches back home.

Some or all of these things may happen in such cases. If they do, they are still not *payments* for a debt, and if that is how they are seen they will be of no effect. Yet if no such responses, or nothing like them, ever occurred there would indeed be something missing: not a legalistic or contractual understanding of the duty to repay debts, but rather a pathetic defensive barrier erected against the *graciousness* of a gift. It is not indebtedness that will have been overlooked, but the graciousness of the giver. In this case, for instance, the greater loss will not have been to that small Ndebele congregation deprived of their visitor's efforts on their behalf to improve their lot; it will have been to the one who received the gift but did not see, who was offered something that might warm a heart and change a life but who could not accept it.

Here we have an image of a different kind of indebtedness, apparently quite different from the death-dealing systems of international economics. Here is a form of relationship that does oblige, but not in the same way. Here is something we can recognise in the relationships we have to parents or friends, and without which life would be greatly impoverished. Sometimes such indebtednesses do not involve money, but then again sometimes they do; parenting, for instance, is not mainly about money, but it certainly involves major financial responsibilities. But then again, would we not find it odd of parents to think of their children in terms of what they had cost? You could, no doubt, draw up an account of how much you owe your parents; but if it ever came to that what kind of relationship would that be? And there are those whose life experience has told them that they will always be people in debt and that they will never be able to repay what they owe. But what kind of life could produce such a response? No doubt the consulting rooms of counsellors and psychiatrists have witnessed many accounts of lives like that.

But such experiences communicate little of what is involved either in wholesome human living or in a real sense of what it is to know God and trust God. 'I am the Lord your God who brought you up out of the land of Egypt; you shall have no other gods but me' is not, surely, the announcement that a debt is now due for payment. It does say something, though, about what it would mean to recognise the experience of release, and what one might hope this would lead to. The release that commandment declares was a piece of untold generosity, and the response of loyalty simply states what it means to have had the experience and recognised it. Like the Corinthians faced with the need of their fellow Christians, they knew they were *also* faced with the truth of a generosity of which they in their turn had been recipients.

We do well, however, not to draw too firm a boundary between debt and gift, and to reflect that what appear to be gifts do also contain expectations and rules about how they are to be made and what response is indicated. What would Christmas be, after all, without gifts; and yet the gifts of Christmas come packaged not only in brightly coloured paper, but in expectations as well:

> The element of ambiguity or paradox in the psychology of the gift is the virtually universal conclusion that gifts are never *merely* gifts. Some kind of reciprocity is nearly always expected. So much of Christmas giving actually shows a more calculated character than is generally acknowledged. There are 'rules', not written down and perhaps not consciously known, that determine with a surprising degree of precision what presents are appropriate, as a function of the occasion, the donor and the recipient. To violate these rules, to give too little, or indeed to give too much, can be insulting.[1]

One obvious set of 'rules' that Burgoyne and Lea go on to highlight is about who may give whom money as a gift: generally it seems only people of higher status may give money to people of a lower status, or age, or place within the family. A gift of money may be welcome from a parent to their offspring at university; but in the reverse direction it will not 'work' as a gift. And the issue of the giving and receiving of money brings with it another point: in some sense it is 'the thought that counts' (although only if the thought does also issue in a present!). One problem about money can be a sense that insufficient attention was given to choosing something, that it is 'impersonal' in the sense that it was not really the result of care expended and affection shown.

Then there is the whole matter also of the 'surprise'; the rituals about wrapping presents up and keeping them secret express the fact that the kind of Christmas present we really relish is the one we had not thought of wishing for, the one that elicits a smile of recognition as we see that someone knew what we should like even better than we did ourselves. So the problem – almost the challenge – of Christmas is that the abundance seems the enemy of the superabundance; the rituals and the expectations somehow have to be transcended or even ingeniously bypassed if the real pleasure of giving and receiving is to be entered into at all.

These are matters of common experience, but also of careful research. Marcel Mauss' famous treatise on *The Gift* relied on research into the customs and rituals of primitive societies,[2] describing the rules, rituals and expectations with great care, but then coming to the conclusion that in the modern world giving is really an archaism, preserved by those with an investment in the maintenance of past customs. David Cheal however makes the point that such a picture leaves out of account what he calls (significantly from the point of view of this study) the 'moral economy', largely operative in the realm of the private and the intimate, and hitherto predominantly an area of life in which women have the main investment: revealing what Cheal calls 'the feminised ideology of love'.[3] The traditionally greater involvement of men in what he calls the 'political economy', what we may call the economy of exchange and of debt, has left the art of gift-giving (as, we may reflect, of hospitality and many other kinds of generosity) to be chiefly the preserve of women. Certainly Cheal's conversations with donors and recipients of gifts reveal just how important and how complex is the art of giving a gift, and just how much significance is carried by the way in which it is received.

The economies of gift and exchange

I have referred already to Nietzsche's comment in *The Genealogy of Morals* that morality began when the first buyer met the first seller, and we have to take seriously the relationship between the economics of gift and exchange, which in some way seem to presuppose each other. The possibility of surprise seems to depend on some baseline of expectation which it exceeds, and the experience of generosity is in relation to something that might have been owed. The economy of gift is always an economy of excess, and the economy of exchange is the one which is exceeded.

We know, for that reason, that a life spent depending on other people's gifts is felt as demeaning; each gift comes with the message that the recipient has nothing to give in return, and that it is not that the world of exchange has had its expectations exceeded by a superabundant generosity but rather that there were no expectations there in the first place. Each 'gift' presented in such circumstances is another step in the destruction of the dignity of the recipient and a testimony to a relationship of

fundamental inequality. We call it paternalism, and none of us
wishes to be on the receiving end of it.

This is no small matter in a world where mass unemployment
is with us (for all the minor fluctuations in the precise figure)
on a scale not seen since the pre-war depression, a world in
which such unemployment is also a global issue because the
competitive export of unemployment has become the positive
strategy of industrialised countries. (We saw earlier that this is
one of the results of the international debt crisis.) Apart from
the political and economic intractability of the problem, the
possibility of large numbers of individuals and households having
to live their lives depending on 'welfare' or 'benefit' – either
word is full of irony given how little such a way of life 'benefits'
anybody's 'welfare' – raises in its sharpest form the question
whether we can dispense with the economy of exchange as part
of the meaning of work and employment.

The issue is articulated with great clarity in the transactions
that take place in the course of the parable of the labourers in
the vineyard (Matthew 20: 1–16). The story is clearly set in the
economy of exchange: 'After agreeing with the [first group of]
labourers for the usual daily wage, [the landowner] sent them
into his vineyard.' And when the owner goes out to find more
workers there is still only the faintest hint that the economy of
exchange may be about to be transcended. Certainly the first
group of labourers had no reason to expect it, for having seen
those hired later receive the full day's wage 'they thought they
would receive more', and when they received the same amount
'they grumbled against the landowner, saying, "These last worked
only one hour, and you have made them equal to us who have
borne the burden of the day and the scorching heat."'

In part the landowner also takes his stand on the proprieties
of the exchange economy too: 'he replied to one of them,
"Friend, I am doing you no wrong; did you not agree with me
for the usual daily wage? Take what belongs to you and go. . . .
Am I not allowed to do what I choose with what belongs to
me?"' The economy of exchange is an economy of contract and
property, and the vineyard is tended within that economy. But
into that economy there breaks another one, and its appearance
is not wholly welcome: ' "I choose to give this last the same as
I give to you. . . . Or are you envious because I am generous?"
So the last will be first and the first last.' So the unpredictability,

the arbitrariness, of the gift economy confronts the economy of exchange to the benefit of those who had had no work for the first part of the day, but to the irritation of those who had.

The generosity occurs within the context supplied by the world of work and contract in which payment is as agreed, and the landowner does not bind himself to do any more than the rules of that world require. Generosity, by contrast, acknowledges no rules, and the economy of gift makes no contracts: 'I will have mercy on whom I will have mercy' (Exodus 33:19, quoted in Romans 9:15). Nobody acquires a right to generosity; the framework of the economy of exchange is the one in which the economy of gift is carried on, but it cannot prescribe its rules or subject it to its contracts.

Nor can the economy of exchange expect to have the last word: 'The first shall be last and the last first' is not a legislative utterance ushering in some new rules for the economy of exchange, a permanent abolition of differentials, as we might say, a severing of the relationship within the world of work between what is done and what is paid. It is a statement about which economy has ultimately to prevail. We are being told that while the gift economy may seem to exist within the exchange economy and to presuppose it, in fact the exchange economy exists by virtue of a gift and will in the end have to acknowledge that truth.

There is a further point too: not only does the exchange economy ultimately exist as a result of the gift of life, but it exercises its rights only on certain conditions. When the manipulation of the economy of exchange produces results that deny justice to the poor, as we have seen in previous chapters, that is precisely the context in which something has to happen to re-establish the priority of the economy of gift and the conditionality of the economy of exchange – and such an upheaval will be greeted (as it was in the vineyard) with the hostility of those with an investment in the operation of the economy of exchange, even those, like these labourers, whose profit from it is small.

So the economies of gift and exchange are related to each other in a complex way: we learn about gift and experience gift because it exceeds what by the rules of exchange we would be entitled to; but it remains true always that the universe is held in life as the result of a gift, and that truth always remains over and above whatever the economy of exchange may deliver. As Paul puts it to the Corinthians (1 Corinthians 4:7), 'What do you have that you did not receive? And if you received it, why do you boast as if it were not a gift?' And as C. F. Evans points out, this fundamental indebtedness is emphatically *not* what the petition in the Lord's Prayer seeks to have remitted, for 'it is one way of describing the permanent relation of creature to Creator, and this relation cannot be dissolved. To seek to dissolve it would itself be sin.'[4] We may add that an economy of exchange which takes on the kind of life of its own – that is, a life not given and received – that I have described in earlier chapters has indeed sought to 'dissolve that relationship' by forsaking the conditionality under which it exists. We know the outcome of the dissolution of that relationship, and shall return in later pages to consider what has to be done to reinstate it.

The gift and the given

First, however, and in the light of Mauss' suspicion of the gift relationship as always, or almost always, expecting a gift in exchange, we need to reflect further on whether and in what way we may say that life is grounded in gift, or that the exchange economy of daily living exists within that fundamental context. After all, we observed earlier that it is possible to suspect any reference to giving of being sheer manipulation, as Graham Shaw for example describes Paul's persuasion of the Corinthians to 'give' to the Church in Jerusalem on the basis that they had received of God's generosity and would receive it again if they in their turn were generous.

At one level we are dealing with the anatomy of human transactions. In beginning to address the question, 'Can a gift be given?', John Milbank raises the question whether all giving is in fact – as a sixteenth-century preacher from whom he quotes discerns in the activities of magistrates who take bribes – 'giffe-gaffe', in effect 'personified mutual help, whose immemorial law is that what is given demands a gift in return'.[5] In examining the notion of gift linguistically, he finds its ambiguous quality in a number of ways. 'Giffe-gaffe' is the old English expression for 'give and take', but the closeness of the two halves of the expression, differing only by one vowel, suggests that there is not much that lies between giving and taking. That the Greek for gift, *dosis*, has come to us in the form of the word 'dose' suggests that gifts can be quite doubtful things to receive (and what about an overdose?).

But most important to his exploration and ours is the strange connection between what is given and what is *a* given – the unquestionable basis of an argument, a 'brute fact'. So as well as the ambiguity about whether there can be such a thing as a real gift (that is, one that does not expect something in return), there is the uncertainty about what is in the most fundamental sense 'given'. We may notice that Bonhoeffer's statement of humanity's having come of age involves living *etsi deus non daretur*, a phrase generally translated 'as if God did not exist' but which would more accurately be rendered 'as if God were not a given'.

It is significant, too, that in current discussion of the fundamentals of ontology, of what there is, the notions of gift and giving have come to be so important. Jacques Derrida and Jean-Luc Marion place great weight on gift, the original 'donation' that is involved in our awareness of the world and of God.[6] John Milbank likewise in his article, 'Can a gift be given?', explores the tension that comes from the fact that a good gift (that is, a thoughtful, well-chosen gift) does always produce some response, at least of gratitude or pleasure. 'However, if gifts are only good according to the measure of concealed moral contracts, debts and obligations, what is a gift after all? What distinguishes it from the fulfilling, albeit the just fulfilling, of a binding contract?'[7] At the human level we have unwritten rules which help us to know whether a gift is really a gift, and to be regarded as such: we should be insulted if the return were instant and very similar to the original gift, for that would lead us to assume that our gift had been regarded as 'giffe-gaffe', an implied contract.

How is this to be related to the structure of Being itself, to the way by which God relates to the world and to the character of the Church, seen as an anticipation of God's purpose for the world? If we are to speak, as I have earlier, of the gift economy as that which contains the exchange economy, and which in a sense gives the exchange economy its sphere of legitimate operation, can we find a means of expressing the gift relationship itself in a way that does not simply make it a part of the world of exchange? To put it at its sharpest, can there really be an 'exchange of gifts'? The question is crucial for that is the kind of body that Paul describes the Church to be. 'The New Testament frequently suggests that unstinting generosity and the cancellation of debts cease to be intermittent, or directed merely to the needy and defaulters, but become the *habitual norm* of a new form of community practice.'[8]

Seen in that light, Paul's words in Romans 13:8, 'Owe no-one anything except to love one another' becomes a remarkable statement of the character of a community founded not on debt but on 'infinitised gift-giving'. Even more, it is founded on the gift received from God, a gift that is prophetic (that is, not immediate, for it looks forward to the fulfilment of all things) and forever new (the same giver giving the same love in ways that are always different). The 'infinite debt' becomes a light burden, for what it requires is not impossible payment but only that loving response which the gift itself draws out of us, once it is 'given', as Milbank says in conclusion, that God is love. That which sustains the world is also its ultimate purpose; and the gift to be anticipated within the life of the community of faith is therefore neither the given of brute fact nor the gift given in expectation of equivalent return, but *true* gift: not a fixing of how the future must be, but an opening out of what it can be – in short, grace not mortgage.

Put thus, the matter seems to be one of great complexity, and what is more somehow beyond our grasp, not just intellectually but even more in terms of practice. Yet we also notice that we are speaking here of a matter of very common knowledge: we have all had sight of the kind of community that moves out of the realm of mere exchange, let alone crippling debt, into real gift exchange and superabundance.

While I was writing this book I was invited to take part in the farewell dinner to two friends who had offered a profound and inspiring image of faithfulness in life and work over three decades. I was asked to give a lecture and endeavoured to convey something of the material in this book about indebtedness. It came to me suddenly, and with great simplicity, that all those present on that occasion had a very clear understanding of the fundamentals of this matter, and it was before our very eyes. What we were gathered for was not to fulfil a contract: no one had promised at the beginning of that long and creative ministry that if it was correctly carried out there would be a farewell dinner to honour it. What had happened was quite simply that all those there had been touched by that ministry with a sense of the superabundant, and of what, even though it came out of a piece of work that had been contracted for, was nevertheless there to be experienced as pure gift.

We also know of occasions, and moments in occasions, when we experience the less exalted sensations that come when what is said to be a gift is not one. If for example people are not properly remunerated for their employment, if their work is taken for granted, then the same dinner party becomes not a gift but an insult; it amounts to the ignoring of an unpaid debt of exchange, reneged on not because it was unjustly or involuntarily incurred, but because some were too mean or too oppressive to carry out the responsibilities they had undertaken. These are situations of which we know from our daily experience: the economy of exchange has been violated, and at that point a gift becomes a mere insult. A tip or a Christmas collection can partake of the nature of a gift; but not if everybody knows it is intended to do duty for unjust pay and conditions.

This book has largely been about the violation of the conditions of the economy of exchange such that it no longer shows that it takes place within the gift economy of God. The violation of the poor at home, of debtor nations abroad, and of the planet we share, are signs of an economy of exchange that does not know itself as inhabiting an economy of gift, that is oblivious to its conditionality, and that is therefore is unable to give and receive genuine gifts, the gifts of God and one another. An economy of exchange that no longer dwells within the realm of gift turns into one in which exchange is itself dishonoured, and in which there is space neither for the gift nor the graciousness that are essential to the experience of God. In such a debased economy all becomes contract, and broken contract at that. It is to such a world that Christ came as Gift from the Giver, as Jubilee from Nazareth, to renew the gift and to call for a response: the remission of the debts that had accrued, the remission of the debts of those who had been violated by an exchange economy that had in its turn forgotten the condition and purpose for which it had been given. As Evans puts it, within the context of the petition for remission in the Lord's Prayer:

What lies here behind the thought of debt is not our

existence as such, but the fact that we exist for something. Life is not simply loaned to us; it is life of a certain kind which is given – and it is given for something. It is the failure to fulfil this something which constitutes the debt.[9]

What was the Giver of all things to do about that debt?

Atonement as transformed economy

So how is the process of amends to begin? What if God himself became human and helped us to achieve reconciliation? To give a modern analogy, it is as though a group of vandals having ruined a pensioner's home – and unable to afford the tools and equipment and lacking the know-how to right the situation – are joined by the pensioner working alongside them. Instead of youths resentful at an externally imposed community service order, the pensioner has become the catalyst for a radically new situation: one in which by his 'mucking in' the guilty youths are transformed from those who feel themselves merely to have 'done their time' into human beings who both desire and know themselves to be forgiven.[10]

Thus the Doctrine Commission of the Church of England offers a contemporary analogy to explain the idea of atonement dominant in Western Christianity since the eleventh-century bishop and theologian, Anselm of Canterbury, expounded it in his *Cur Deus Homo*. The coming of Christ is God's gift into a situation of the desperate need of humanity to find some means of reparation in the face of its debt of sin. So the Commission continues:

Through his embodiedness [God] was able to offer a life of perfect obedience and thus make perfect amends, a life which can now empower our own feeble efforts at amends as they are transformed through his ever-present life in us as the head of his continuing embodiedness, the Church.

Anselm's view has been immensely influential, though at the time it was propounded it was strongly resisted by another view that has since commended itself to those who have found any idea of the satisfaction of human indebtedness to God objectionable. Abelard saw the death of Christ as a unique example of God's love for alienated humankind, and at the same time as an example of a human life lived in perfect obedience. His objection to Anselm's account of Christ's death as a satisfaction echoes the feelings of many who have encountered the various versions of it in subsequent generations:

> How cruel and wicked it seems that anyone should demand the blood of an innocent person as the price for anything, or that it should in any way please him that an innocent man should be slain – still less that God should consider the death of his Son so agreeable that by it he should be reconciled to the whole world![11]

Yet we have to ask what such theories have to say to the particular structures of sin with which we have been concerned hitherto. In particular, what do they say to a world in captivity to a credit and debt economy that is out of effective control and that is experiencing subjugation to the power of global money, a subjugation experienced not only by the victims of chronic indebtedness but also by the world's creditor nations and by individuals who can see no way of escape from the means by which they now profit? Are we to suppose, as the explanatory analogy rather suggests we might, that it is principally the *debtors* who need rescue? And that the arrival of aid teams from creditor countries to live alongside the poor of the Third World or the impoverished of our own society enables them to be relieved of the burden of debt? To speak in the terms of the analogy, is the indebtedness really only that of the youths convicted of vandalism? What of the responsibility of the adult community for a world of unemployment and hopelessness out of which such behaviour is often born?

Something within us continues to cry out against this God who came alongside us out of pure love. Is there not a divine responsibility for the shape of the world? And is the suffering already present in the world not sufficient reparation? In her remarkable exploration, *Deadly Innocence*, Angela West gives voice to these outraged objections in words that could be used within the circles of present-day feminism:

> Why should it be necessary for sin to be paid for, we ask? Isn't God supposed to be almighty and all loving? Why

shouldn't God forgive us our sins without any 'payment' –
especially as in our case, being women, our sins are of a
lesser order than men's? And anyway, what about God's
mercy? God's mercy is supposed to be endlessly available.
This doesn't really square up with God allowing God's son
to be crucified for our sins. It's a barbaric medieval idea
which in our enlightened times we really don't need.[12]

In her own thinking, West comes to be very critical of this
particular feminist critique; my purpose in quoting it is to illustrate from that perspective what could be, and has been,
articulated from other perspectives. What are the various ranks
of the world's poor to make of being constantly told of this
beneficent God who deals with their debt by making amends
on their behalf through inflicting further suffering on his own
son? Does such a doctrine really attend adequately to the deep
dislocation in the human economy and its effects on those who
bear a totally disproportionate load of the world's sufferings? It
is significant that West includes this expression of outrage in a
chapter entitled 'Debt and redemption', in which, as well as the
huge statistical burden of world debt, she places before herself
and her readers the life of the *Good Woman of Bangkok*, Aoi, and
Denis O'Rourke, who made a film of her life, and who
attempted to buy her out of the slavery in which she found
herself – and failed.

That story raises for her in the most basic way how redemption
is possible. In the end her conclusion is that the Christian story,
its doctrine of redemption through Christ, has in fact more to
offer than those outraged objections are able to recognise. She
comes to that point by taking seriously what, from a feminist
point of view, has been a further strong objection to the Christian
story of redemption: simply, how can women be saved by a man?
This, the issue of Christ's *difference*, she then makes central to her
exposition. He is indeed 'other', and not of course just in terms
of gender: he is other in time, in race, in circumstances. He is
the centre of the

narrative of faith [that] requires us to believe that this debt
was paid once and for all by a Jewish male who was tortured
to death in the first century – in once sense a victim so
ordinary it could have been anyone. Yet this obscure indi-

vidual was raised from death by God and 'will come again in glory'.[13]

The Christ of faith comes in the person of the Other, the one who was one of us but not by being a member of any of the groups into which we divide ourselves in order to persuade ourselves that we are not the ones who need redeeming, that we have paid for our bit. 'This God is certainly not in our image', West continues,

> and that is the point. The task of Christian preaching is to remind whoever is tempted to forget it that God cannot be made in our image. So as God is to us twentieth-century women so God is to all men and all women. God is not of our gender, nor of the opposite gender. For God does not personify maleness either and undermines the claims of arrogant men, including men in the Church, as well as women who seek a share in their power. But God is the God of those without defences, either practical or theoretical, in a patriarchal society.[14]

So Christ is redeemer. But was that by paying the debt for us?

Since in speaking of Christ's saving work we are speaking of matters that can only be approached by metaphor and illustration, it is worth asking how the value of a metaphor is to be assessed. It was a key aspect of the agenda of this book to seek the recovery of a connectedness between the language of faith and the secular reality faced by human beings, and in particular by human beings in their strength – Bonhoeffer's two criteria. What would be the effect, in relation to these two criteria, of continuing to speak of Christ as paying for human beings a debt to the Father?

In fairness I need to dissociate such a view from some of its more lurid representations in theories of *penal* substitution, which suggest that God actively *punished* Jesus for human transgression and have wrongly caused people to reach a negative judgement about any way of speaking of atonement that involves the satisfaction of a debt owed to the Father. If my concern had been to pursue Bonhoeffer's question about who Christ is for us in relation to policies for dealing with crime I should have had to take such ways of presenting the atonement in much more detail, as we find for instance in Timothy Gorringe's *God's Just Vengeance*.[15]

Yet as Gorringe does in relation to crime and punishment, we cannot avoid asking, in terms of the economic concerns that have appeared in our exploration hitherto, what would be the effect, in terms of piety as well as politics, of presenting Calvary as the payment of a debt? In terms of piety, the person who is told that she was indebted to the Father with a debt beyond repayment, and that this debt has been paid by means of a satisfaction provided by God himself in the person of his crucified Son, may believe that she has thereby been set free. But her thankfulness may not affect her sense of indebtedness at a sufficiently deep level to offer a genuine sense of freedom. After all, are we not doubly indebted if, having been burdened with a debt that cannot be paid that debt is then paid for us? It must be doubtful whether seeing satisfaction in this way really confers the gift of freedom it is designed to convey.

What then of the social and political effects of such an account? To whom, first of all, does such an account make its principal address? Clearly we can see that such an account speaks both to creditors and debtors: to the former about mercy and to the latter about the need for the payment of their debts (for if God demands some payment, even if himself supplying it, the principle of the payment of debts, even ones beyond repayment, is affirmed). But the primary audience for such an account must be deemed to be those who might end up, or already have ended up, in debt. When the Revd Greville Ewing entered the pulpit in Nile Street Meeting House, Glasgow, in March 1821 he was quite clear on the point:

> Debt is so great an evil, that in the holy scriptures, it is used as one of the principal similitudes for explaining the nature of sin; from which, unless there were provided a divine satisfaction and forgiveness according to the gospel of Christ, there could be no salvation.... What is the meaning of his pathetic lamentation, when, introduced as speaking in his own person, he exclaimed, 'Save me, O God; for the waters are come in unto my soul?' – He was paying debt.[16]

The preacher's exegesis of Romans 13:8 is literally to 'owe no one anything' – unless you absolutely have to because you are in need, and then you must pay as soon as you can. The connection between the atonement and business probity, that is above all in the payment of debts, is clear in such an extract; and in his account of *The Age of Atonement*, Boyd Hilton shows how very strong was the connection between the emergent code of business practice in the late eighteenth and early nineteenth centuries and in the doctrine of the atonement.[17] So it was that, as Tawney also chronicled, a biblical tradition involving severe controls on lending came to be changed so as to support the lender and encourage the faithful discharge of debts. In the service of that the economy of salvation is presented as an address to the personal religious needs of its hearers geared primarily to assisting them in their weakness.

The relationship between atonement and economics is one instance of the way in which an economy of salvation set forth at a time when the Church was, and expected to be, over against the world, had to be adjusted, in this case radically adjusted, to a post-Constantinian situation in which the Church and the world were seen as essentially coterminous. Denny Weaver demonstrates how it became far more appropriate for the Church – which had represented salvation as God's victory over the devil through Christ's resurrection from death, as the Fathers spoke of it, or *Christus Victor*, as Gustav Aulén named it[18] – to speak in the situation of post-Constantinian Christendom in ways that did not involve criticism of the social order.

The absence of a social component to salvation fits precisely with the Constantinian church. Since the church has come to coincide with the dominant society, the church has lost the sense that salvation needs to have a social dimension. Stated another way, since the society is assumed to be Christian, the idea disappears from view that the work of Christ envisions the transformation of institutions as well as individuals. Since the society as a whole has been declared Christian, no perceived need exists to declare salvation as social, and the focus on individuals and the individualization and personalization of sin and salvation follows as a natural consequence.[19]

Specifically in relation to the economy of our world, it has been my concern in this book to say that we have arrived at a point where the world and national economies cannot be declared just, let alone Christian, in their outworking. That means that human beings, and specifically those who profess

Christian faith, have to make a decision whether or not they will continue to collude with structures that so manifestly destroy life and elevate money from being an instrument to being a divinity.

To decide to say 'no' to such structures involves activity at a number of levels. In the course of writing this book I have been privileged to come to know those who are inventing alternative structures like credit unions which will enable lending and borrowing to become humane again, even while others give time and attention to advising those who are the victims of the present system. I have also come to know, and have earlier referred to, those who are engaged in the political struggle to secure some remission of the debt owed by the poorest countries. These and many other actions are required of those who decide that they cannot collude any longer.

But at another level it is also vital that we avoid the use of our most basic religious language in ways that support such collusion, and I have suggested that the language of Christ's 'paying a debt to the Father on our behalf' is more likely to do now what it has done in the past, namely support structures of economic oppression. I have suggested also that the content of his preaching and the character of his ministry speak to us rather of economic transformation than of accommodation within the system. We are invited out of the economy that destroys life into one that gives it. Like the servant in the parable who was forgiven a large debt yet refused to remit a small one, we resist this invitation: we thankfully receive the remission we know we need, but are unwilling to accept that this is the token of a policy change, and that we are now in a new economy in which forgiveness is not a one-off transaction for the desperate but a way of life to be expressed in every part of the believer's life and the life of the believing community; 'forgive us as we forgive'.

Those who would serve such a new economy have to be clear of the price involved in its transformation, even though they may try to make progress without paying it. But ultimately the economy of credit and debt, the economy in service to money, is a violent one; nobody watching the deployment of the military strength of Western nations should be in any doubt that in the end creditors will pursue their debts, and even before they pursue them militarily the economic system is already demanding its victims every day.

The total commitment of Christ to that transformation of the economy therefore had to involve his violent death. As René Girard puts it, 'Violence is unable to bear the presence of a being that owes it nothing – that pays it no homage and threatens its kingship in the only way possible.' The world of violence, economic and military-in-support-of-economic, reveals its essential nature in the act of violence: its total commitment to securing its ends. And yet the fate of the totally committed one, Christ, in his pursuit of the new economy is ultimately the source of renewal. He does not pay the debt; he ushers in the order that will make such death-dealing indebtedness a thing of the past.

> We can see why the Passion is found between the preaching of the Kingdom and the Apocalypse. . . . [I]t is a phenomenon that has no importance in the eyes of the world – incapable, at least in principle, of setting up or reinstating a cultural order, but very effective, in spite of those who know better, in carrying out subversion. In the long run, it is quite capable of undermining and overturning the whole cultural order and supplying the secret motive force of all subsequent history.[20]

Such is the account we need of the death of Christ, a death as the result of his life and the essential and uniquely necessary enactment of the pursuit of the new economy of freedom from the power of debt. It is a death understandable in relation to the Kingdom of God for which Jesus taught us to pray and live, and for which he lived totally. This death was the event that issued not in a payment-on-behalf, but in the creation of a community that could experience his life restored and be the movement empowered by 'the secret motive force of all subsequent history', expressed in a common life fashioned as a structure of anticipation: the hope of a world where debt will not rule.

The Church as celebration of freedom

As this exploration nears its conclusion, something more needs to be said about how the Church might express in its own life that anticipation of the Kingdom of God not subject to the power of debt that the previous section declares to be the effect of Christ's saving work. As Dan Hardy remarked in responding to the contrast made in Chapter 4 between the way of love and the way of debt, the Church 'is far from even recognising the theological significance of its own economic realities'. He continues with a challenge:

> . . . [H]ow the church can enable a dynamic growth to mutual love and hope is a question which needs a good deal more attention. Although mutuality and equality are *minima*, radical trust, love and hope conferred by each on others will be hard won, and require drawing directly on the redemption of Jesus Christ.[21]

Clearly the attention that it needs will demand all the sensitivity and pastoral skill we have and more. It will require a re-visioning of our language along the lines I have tried to suggest, and that needs to be allowed to affect every aspect of the Church's life. First of all, however, it will require the breaking of a long and destructive silence within the Church's life about the matter of money. 'When I came to this country it was the first time I felt ashamed to be poor in church', said a friend recently, in a sentence that makes a severe judgement on that silence. Could a local church imagine getting to grips with the task of sharing the hardships, embarrassments, and feelings of guilt that surround this topic?

Certainly it has had no encouragement to do so from a denomination such as my own which has dealt with financial difficulties in recent years not by reflection on the 'theological significance of its own economic realities' but by an immediate resort to precisely the methods that would be used in any secular concern that found itself in financial trouble: retrenchment and calls for redoubled effort along the same lines as hitherto. The absence of such reflection in times of difficulty makes it clear that there is no tradition of reflection on what it means for the Church, any church, to engage with the economic powers. It has been assumed that a few concessions to uneasy consciences – avoiding blatant (though not always covert) investment in arms or gambling – deals with this matter.

Patterns of leadership in the centres of power in the Church and patterns of congregational life interact with one another: if it is thought at congregational level that serious reflection on its economic engagement is not required of the Church, and that the role of the congregation in relation to money is simply to raise as much of it as possible, then there will be no energy or attention left to bring our economic relationships with each other out into the open. And if the congregations are not places where involvement with the economy is the subject of careful, prayerful and mutual conversation, confession and intercession, it will be felt in the centres of power that congregations have to be regarded as sources of funds rather than of insight and critical judgement.

The silence has to be broken. For years I have received and given spiritual direction, and have to say by way of confession that money has hardly figured; and I have gently broken enough silences to know that I am not alone in that experience. In years of attending worship and of preaching at it, I again have to admit that money seems to figure only when it is time to raise the question of 'Christian giving'; whenever the issue is raised it therefore arouses the instant defences of those who suspect, usually rightly, that they are about to be confronted with the Church in self-serving rather than world-serving mode.

At the centre of this breaking of silence must be the matter of that which is primarily constitutive of the Church's life, its 'secret motive force', and that is its worship. For that is the point at which we act out in our shared life the dynamic of the Kingdom of forgiveness which enables mutual trust. We gather, after all, to celebrate pure gift, the act of God the Father, out of love and only love, in creating the world in freedom; the act of God the Son, out of love and only love, in restoring the economy of freedom; the act of the Holy Spirit, love and only love, in animating the Body of Christ in its freedom of response. We do not come to wait upon our demanding creditor or to make our expected downpayments by the due date. What we are invited into is a context where our response may simply reflect as much as, and no more than, that 'out of love and only love' which is the character of God's action and is hoped for from those who have received it.

For the action of the Church, all its prayer and most of all its eucharists, are its response in kind to that freedom of gift by which it was constituted. To receive that gift is at the same time to be drawn into a response. Such worship is enlivened when it

is undertaken by a community that has decided out of its awareness of the gift of Christ that it will collude with the domination
of debt no longer. The idol will have been named at last, and
with all the sacrifices that that idol has demanded.

Above all, a church which sees that dynamic in its worship
will begin to be able to confront the *conditionality* that a world
bound by debt imposes as a condition for belonging, and the
guilt that results from this conditionality is the way in which
the notion of debt acquires its capacity to spread its power
through every aspect of life, subverting the desire for truth and
love and turning it into a debt. Richard Fenn describes the
process in this way, as he writes his challenge to the Church to
deal with the dynamic of sin and forgiveness in the light of its
apprehension of God:

> Social life exploits this sense of an unsatisfied longing or
> debt; the sense of indebtedness becomes a diffuse feeling of
> obligation and underlies a willingness to take social life
> seriously. The desire for something 'more' becomes a sense
> that something more is demanded of the self. . . . [T]he
> self that feels owed comes to feel indebted.[22]

If that kind of indebtedness is one result of failing to apprehend
the radical freedom of God, the result of being a church in
which the silence about debt is broken will be that the church
will find itself able to rebuild the mutual trust in which the wide
range of feelings of indebtedness, deriving much of their power
from the silence about monetary debt, which come in the form
of all kinds of guilt, can be faced. Robert Farrar Capon puts his
vision of the result with characteristic bluntness, reflecting on a
piece of spiritual counsel he has offered to 'Helen':

> And therefore, since the gracious work of Christ Jesus is
> already in everybody and for everybody simply because he's
> the God who holds everything in his loving, forgiving
> hands, the root premise of my counsel to Helen was just
> this: *the guilt shop has been closed*, boarded up entirely and
> for good by God's grace and nothing else. All she needs to
> do is trust that million-dollar news and let the liberating
> relationship it has already established happen. *She never has
> to spend another penny in the guilt department.*[23]

The emphasis is the author's – as is his estimate of the monetary value of the news!

Such a Church, which refreshes its own grasp on its own beginning in forgiveness as an anticipation of a world not held down by debt, will be empowered to address another aspect of conditionality as well: its constant tendency to erect barriers, conditions for belonging, as a result of which it has a long and terrible history of colluding with the world's patterns of discrimination and oppression.[24] Once we have faced together our domination by the economy of credit and debt, we approach others without requiring them to meet our conditions, with a future opened up by grace rather than closed by mortgage. So having unmasked an idol we cease in the name of that idol to demand its sacrifices from others, and the Church itself becomes and builds structures of anticipation that look forward to an economy of freedom.

Conclusion: The promise of freedom

This book started out with a question, 'Who really is Jesus Christ for us today?' Many of those interested in that question would find it odd to be drawn into the world of trade and money in the search for an answer. So accustomed are we to a purely personal reference for our language of faith that such concerns tend to be ones that we take up only with what energy we have left. I hope those who began with that kind of scepticism will, like many others with whom I have discussed these questions in the course of writing this book, have come to see that the world of money is indeed a place where we have to look.

For it is a world to which in varying degrees we are all in captivity, and through which we condemn (usually unwittingly) many of our fellow human beings, and the world we inhabit, to a future under mortgage. In the process we also condemn (again often unwittingly) our Christian life and language to a privatisation and ultimately to an irrelevance which dishonour the life we are claiming to live and the Christ whom we claim to follow. That world does, it turns out, have the capacity to ask us those questions from Bonhoeffer – about our identity, about our discernment and about the limits of our solidarity – that the question of Christ needs to ask of us if it is to receive an authentic answer. There are many friends and colleagues, as well as countless others unknown to me, who have already begun for themselves, and in the campaigns in which they are involved, to engage with the injustice of the debt economy, and I hope they have been refreshed by the sense that what they are engaged with is money but more than money: it is with the shape of life promised in the Kingdom of God.

There will be others, and maybe not many of them will read this book, for whom it also matters to me deeply that the connections I have made make sense. It is probably true that not many of the most serious victims of debt will read this, as probably also not many will read it for whom the Christian message has been for too long a remote and unreal matter, disconnected from those things that most deeply affect human life in our time. If by chance there are such among the readers of this book, and if they have persevered to this point, through those chapters which still have about them much of the private language of the Christian community, I hope that they too may have found that their own concern with what they and others owe and cannot repay has its place not just deep in the traditions of the Christian community, but in the life of the one who brought it into being. Those who engage with the business of economic transformation, which is the opening of the world to justice and the freeing of the world to a future of hope, are in my view doing work that is not just good but sacred: they share in the dynamic of life towards grace and the redeeming of its mortgages.

And that dynamic has its roots in the universe's gracious beginning in freedom, the gracious restoration of that freedom in Jesus Christ, and the offer of life in the freedom of the Spirit. So I believe; and if the language in which I express that belief is indeed the language of the Christian community, that is because I know no other in which to express my further conviction: that the work of redemption, of unmortgaging the future, is work of ultimate significance, of importance beyond measure, and sustained by the resources of grace it needs.

Notes

Chapter 1: What this book is and how it happened

1. Dietrich Bonhoeffer, *Letters and Papers from Prison*, enlarged edition (London, SCM, 1971), p. 279.
2. ibid. p. 300.
3. Friedrich Nietzsche, *A Genealogy of Morals* (T. Fisher Unwin, 1899), Second Essay, p. 81.
4. See for example the series of studies aptly entitled *World on Loan* by John D. Davies (London, Bible Society, 1993).

Chapter 2: Regain your whole image

1. 'The Past' (*Vergangenheit*), in Bonhoeffer, *Letters and Papers from Prison*, pp. 320–3. See also Dietrich Bonhoeffer and Maria von Wedemeyer, *Love Letters from Cell 92* (London, Harper Collins, 1994), pp. 210–13.
2. Bonhoeffer, *Letters and Papers from Prison*, p. 279.
3. Dietrich Bonhoeffer, *Sanctorum Communio: a dogmatic inquiry into the sociology of the church* (London, Collins, 1963), pp. 111 ff.
4. 'Jesus Christ and the essence of Christianity', address of 11 December 1928 in G. B. Kelly and F. B. Nelson (eds.), *A Testament to Freedom* (London, Harper, 1990), p. 53.
5. 'Bonhoeffer in South Africa', an explanatory essay in Eberhard Bethge, *Bonhoeffer: exile and martyr* (London, Collins, 1975), p. 41.
6. ibid. p. 42.
7. John W. de Gruchy (ed.), *Dietrich Bonhoeffer: witness to Jesus Christ* (London, Collins, 1988), p. 36.
8. David Jenkins, 'Concerning theism' in John A. T. Robinson and David L. Edwards (eds.), *The Honest to God Debate* (London, SCM, 1963).
9. Jenkins was not of course primarily referring to the Bonhoeffer component in Robinson's theology but rather to the extensive use of Tillich's categories, 'ground of being' and 'ultimate reality'. In any case I have since learned better (as have many others), and am glad to acknowledge his invaluable support in the process of writing this book.

10. A. M. Ramsey, Sermon, 24 July 1967, to the Modern Churchmen's Conference held at Somerville College, Oxford, 24–8 July 1967, in *Christ for Us Today: Papers from the Fiftieth Annual Conference of Modern Churchmen* (London, SCM, 1968), p. 12.
11. John W. de Gruchy, *Christianity and Democracy* (Cambridge, Cambridge University Press, 1995), pp. 25 ff.
12. Dietrich Bonhoeffer, *Christology* (London, Collins, 1966), p. 106.
13. ibid. p. 111.
14. ibid. pp. 30 ff.
15. ibid. p. 35.
16. ibid. p. 36.
17. Oscar Cullmann, *Christ and Time* (first published in German, 1946; revised English edition, London, SCM, 1962), p. 17.
18. From the letter of 21 July 1944, quoted in Haddon Willmer, 'Bonhoeffer's sanctity as a problem for Bonhoeffer studies' in *Celebrating Critical Awareness: Bonhoeffer and Bradford 60 years on* (privately printed, International Bonhoeffer Society, Barton Vicarage, Cambridge, 1993).
19. Simon Phipps, unpublished ordination sermon, June 1990. I am grateful to Bishop Phipps both for a very significant address, and for refreshing my memory with his notes.
20. See for instance John W. de Gruchy, *Bonhoeffer and South Africa: theology in dialogue* (Grand Rapids, Eerdmans, 1984).
21. See Eberhard Bethge, *Dietrich Bonhoeffer: a biography* (London, Collins, 1970), pp. 109 ff.
22. See Keith Clements, *A Patriotism for Today: love of country in dialogue with Dietrich Bonhoeffer* (London, Collins, 1986).
23. Bonhoeffer, *Letters and Papers*, p. 285.

Chapter 3: A mountain to move

1. National Consumer Council, *Credit and Debt: the consumer interest* (London, HMSO, 1990), p. vii.
2. Statistics drawn from the introduction to Michael Wolfe, *Handbook of Debt Advice* (London, Child Poverty Action Group, 1996).
3. See also Russell Mannion, *Dealing with Debt: an evaluation of money advice services* (London, HMSO, 1992), p. 11.
4. Figures from the Council of Mortgage Lenders, cited ibid. p. 11.
5. National Consumer Council, *Consumers and Credit* (London, HMSO, 1980), quoted in National Consumer Council, *Credit and Debt*, p. xi.
6. From Alison MacDonald, 'Down and out in Hawthorn Avenue', *Woman* (9 March 1985), quoted in John Doling, Janet Ford and Bruce Stafford, *The Property Owing Democracy* (Aldershot, Gower, 1988), p. 179.

7. Doling *et al.*, *Property Owing Democracy*, p. 5.

8. N. Finnis, writing in 1978, quoted in Doling *et al.*, *Property Owing Democracy*, p. 7.

9. N. Finnis, 'Mortgage arrears: tomorrow's problems' in *Roof* (January 1978, pp. 11–12).

10. Doling *et al.*, *Property Owing Democracy*, p. 9. This includes a table showing the rapid increase in publications relating to the issue of arrears. For a fuller bibliography, see John Doling and Bruce Stafford, *Home Ownership: the diversity of experience* (Aldershot, Gower, 1989), pp. 157 ff.

11. See Doling and Stafford, *Home Ownership: the diversity of experience*, ch. 5.

12. Richard Davis and Yvonne Dhooge, *Living with Mortgage Arrears* (London, HMSO, 1993), p. 45.

13. Doling *et al.*, *Property Owing Democracy*, p. 6.

14. Janet Ford, *The Indebted Society: credit and default in the 1980s* (London, Routledge, 1988), pp. 106–12.

15. Doling *et al.*, *Property Owing Democracy*, p. 6.

16. Lyn C. Thomas, 'A management science perspective' in Andrew R. Morton (ed.), *Domestic Debt: disease of consumer society* (Edinburgh, Centre for Theology and Public Issues, 1996), pp. 33–40.

17. Graham Blount, *A Theology of Social Justice and Forgiveness in an Economic Context (Debt)* (University of Edinburgh, unpublished PhD thesis, 1995), pp. 10 ff. In quoting Graham Blount's work I have been able to make use of this thesis; for a briefer, published account of some of his work on this issue, see Graham K. Blount, 'Sketching the problems and assessing responses: discipline, advice or forgiveness – what do debtors need?' in Morton, *Domestic Debt*, pp. 6–18.

18. Crowther Report, *Consumer Credit* (London, HMSO, 1971), para. 3.7.1.

19. Michael Schluter and David Lee, *Credit and Debt: sorting it out* (London, Marshall Pickering, 1989).

20. See, for instance, Brian Williams, *Cleaning up the Debt Environment: policies for the prevention of debt among low-income families* (Cambridge, Jubilee Centre, 1990).

21. Jubilee Trust, *Escaping the Debt Trap: the problem of consumer credit and debt in Britain today* (Cambridge, Jubilee Centre, 1990).

22. ibid. p. 1.

23. ibid. p. 3.

24. *Report of the Student Money Matters Project* (London, University of Exeter/National Westminster Bank, 1994).

25. Emma Davies and Stephen E. G. Lea, 'Student attitudes to student debt', *Journal of Economic Psychology* 16 (1995), p. 678.

26. Stephen E. G. Lea, Paul Webley and Catherine M. Walker,

'Psychological factors in consumer debt: money management, economic socialization, and credit use', *Journal of Economic Psychology* 16 (1995), p. 700.

27. National Association of Citizens' Advice Bureaux, *The Cost of Living: CAB evidence on debt and poverty* (1992), p. 2.

28. ibid. p. 57.

29. ibid. p. 37.

30. See for example the resource pack *An Introduction to Credit Unions* (Milton Keynes, Open University, 1991), a pack to help groups in the community who are thinking about setting up a credit union. See also Association of British Credit Unions, *Starting a Credit Union* and *Credit Union and You* (London, ABCU, undated).

31. See Richard Berthoud and Teresa Hinton, *Credit Unions in the United Kingdom*, Research Report 693 (Policy Studies Unit, London, 1989).

32. ibid. p. 119.

33. See Ulrich Duchrow, *Alternatives to Global Capitalism* (Utrecht, International Books, 1995), chart on p. 91.

34. *The Independent*, 31 August 1995, quoted by John Miller, Castlemilk East Parish leaflet.

Chapter 4: Loving and owing

1. See Daniel Hardy, 'Created and redeemed sociality', in D. W. Hardy and C. E. Gunton (eds.), *On Being the Church: essays on Christian community* (Edinburgh, T. & T. Clark, 1989), pp. 21–47.

2. Anders Nygren, *Agape and Eros*, trans. Philip S. Watson, (London, SPCK, 1982), pp. 133 ff.

3. ibid. p. 137.

4. ibid. p. 141.

5. I have written elsewhere on the significance of the possibility of radical disappointment for urban living; see Peter Selby, 'Saved through hope', *Christian Action Journal* (Summer 1986), pp. 17–26.

6. David F. Ford, 'Faith in the cities: Corinth and the modern city', *On Being the Church*, p. 243.

7. *Faith in the City: the report of the Archbishop's Commission on Urban Priority Areas* (London, Church Information Office, 1985). Cf. Ford, 'Faith in the cities', pp. 225–30, 246–9, 254 ff.

8. See Selby, 'Saved through hope', pp. 23 ff.

9. Hardy, 'Created and redeemed sociality', p. 22.

10. I am grateful to Alan Laurie for informing me of this and for providing me with a copy of Mrs Phillips' original rules.

11. Jacques Ellul, *The Meaning of the City* (Grand Rapids, Eerdmans, 1970), p. 54.

12. Beatrix Campbell, *Goliath: Britain's dangerous places* (London, Methuen, 1993), p. 257.
13. ibid., p. 269.
14. Hardy, 'Created and redeemed sociality', p. 28.
15. Daniel W. Hardy, 'A magnificent complexity' in David F. Ford and Dennis L. Stamps (eds.), *Essentials of Christian Community* (Edinburgh, T. & T. Clark, 1996), p. 326.

Chapter 5: A world in debt

1. From *The State of the World's Children* (UNICEF, 1989) quoted in Christian Aid, *Banking on the Poor: the ethics of Third World debt* (London, Christian Aid, 1991), pp. 21 ff.
2. S. C. Gwynne, 'Adventures in the loan trade', *Harper's* magazine (September 1988), pp. 22–6, quoted in Susan George, *A Fate Worse than Debt: a radical analysis of the Third World debt crisis* (Harmondsworth, Penguin, 1994), p. 31.
3. There is a debate about precisely how much; but even the lowest possible amount is unsustainable; see George, *A Fate Worse than Debt*, p. 28.
4. M. P. Joseph, 'A Third World viewpoint', *Third World Debt – First World Responsibility* (Edinburgh, Centre for Theology and Public Issues, 1991), p. 12.
5. See for example Ann Pettifor, *Debt: the most potent form of slavery* (London, Debt Crisis Network, 1996).
6. See Susan George and Fabrizio Sabelli, *Faith and Credit: the World Bank's secular empire* (Harmondsworth, Penguin, 1994), p. 88.
7. Susan George, *The Debt Boomerang: how Third World debt harms us all* (London, Pluto Press, 1992), p. 171.
8. Joseph, 'A Third World viewpoint', p. 11.
9. George, *A Fate Worse than Debt*, from the foreword to the updated edition, p. x.
10. ibid. p. 270.
11. Interview for *La Liberté* (9 October 1985), reprinted in Déclaration de Berne, *Pour un développement solidaire*, no. 81 (November 1985); also quoted in George, *A Fate Worse than Debt*, p. 138.
12. See the report by David Copley and Paul Spray, *Who God Bless, Let No Man Curse – Jamaica: health and debt* (London, Christian Aid, 1995).
13. Omar Davies, Finance Minister of Jamaica, quoted in John Jackson's report, *Sacrificing the Future: structural adjustment in Jamaica* (London, Christian Aid, 1995).
14. See George, *A Fate Worse than Debt*, p. 22.
15. See George and Sabelli, *Faith and Credit*.
16. Mark Anderson, international economist of the American Feder-

ation of Labor and Congress of Industrial Organizations, speaking
before a US House of Representatives, June 1990, quoted in
George, *The Debt Boomerang*, p. 26.

17. George, *The Debt Boomerang*, pp. 10 ff.
18. ibid. pp. 32 ff.
19. *IMF Survey* (11 December 1989), p. 370, quoted in George, *The Debt Boomerang*, p. 46; my emphasis.
20. For example the so-called 'Brady deals' whereby the United States government bought in at a discount debts which were unlikely to be repaid from the banks which had made the loans. For an account of the results of this in 1993–4, see M. J. Dent, *Jubilee 2000 and Lessons of the World Debt Tables (1992–93 and 1993–94)* (published by the author, who is co-Chair of Jubilee 2000, Department of Politics, Keele University, 1994) pp. 19 ff.
21. For graphic and detailed accounts of how this is working out in the international debt market, see George, 'The third boomerang: how northern taxpayers are bailing out the banks', *The Debt Boomerang*, pp. 63–92.
22. ibid., 'The fifth boomerang: immigration', pp. 110–35.
23. ibid., Dan Smith, 'The sixth boomerang: conflict and war', pp. 136–67.
24. ibid. p. 144.
25. ibid. pp. 155 ff.
26. ibid. pp. 156–58.
27. ibid. p. 139.
28. ibid. p. 136.

Chapter 6: Everything, even money, has a price

1. Paul Spray, 'The abolition of the international debt trade' in *Third World Debt – First World Responsibility* (Edinburgh, Centre for Theology and Public Issues, 1991), p. 20. The same parallel is drawn by Ann Pettifor, using John Davies' title *A World on Loan*, in a paper, 'Debt: the most potent form of slavery' (London, Debt Crisis Network, 1995) and in her submission to the 1996 Bossey Conference on Jubilee, 'Jubilee and the remission of debts: the Churches and a new fight against slavery'.
2. From Olaudah Equiano's autobiography; see Paul Edwards and David Dabydeen (eds.) *Black Writers in Britain 1760–1890: an anthology* (Edinburgh, Edinburgh University Press 1991, reprinted 1995).
3. Susan George and Fabrizio Sabelli, *Faith and Credit: the World Bank's secular empire* (Harmondsworth, Penguin, 1994), p. 88.
4. Cardinal Roger Etchegaray, President of the Pontifical Council for Justice and Peace and of the Central Committee for the Great

Jubilee of the Year 2000, *Millennium Jubilee: Church event – challenge to society*, the tenth Pope John Paul VI Memorial Lecture (London, CAFOD, 1996).

5. Martin J. Dent, 'Theological help in an urgent economic crisis', *Crucible* (January–March 1994), p. 25.

6. This point is particularly stressed in an unpublished lecture by Bishop Ronald Bowlby, 'Third World debt: what are the ethical issues?' (Essex University, January 1996).

7. Martin J. Dent, 'The debt tables of the World Bank', *Journal of Modern African Studies* 32.4 (1994), p. 697.

8. Papers and reflections from this consultation can be obtained either through the World Council of Churches or through the Debt Crisis Network via the offices of Christian Aid.

9. Susan George, *A Fate Worse than Debt: a radical analysis of the Third World debt crisis* (Harmondsworth, Penguin, 1994), pp. 229–62.

10. Michael Taylor, *Not Angels but Agencies: the ecumenical response to poverty – a primer* (London, SCM Press, 1995), p. 169.

11. Theodor Bovet, *That They May Have Life: a handbook on pastoral care for Christian ministers and laymen* (London, DLT, 1964; trans. J. A. Baker from *Lebendige Seelsorge*, Verlag Paul Haupt, 1951), p. 81.

12. ibid. p. 81.

13. ibid.

14. Georg Simmel, *The Philosophy of Money* (London, Routledge & Kegan Paul, 1978; trans. Tom Bottomore and David Frisby from *Philosophie des Geldes*, Berlin, 1907), p. 236.

15. ibid. p. 401.

16. Nigel Dodd, *The Sociology of Money: economics, reason and contemporary society* (New York, Continuum, 1994), p. 49.

17. See chart in Ulrich Duchrow, *Alternatives to Global Capitalism: drawn from biblical history, designed for political action* (Utrecht, International Books, 1995) p. 91, drawing on the work of H. Creutz.

18. Alan Duncan and Dominic Hobson, *Saturn's Children: how the state devours liberty, prosperity and virtue* (London, Sinclair-Stevenson, 1995), p. 297; my emphasis.

19. Michael Novak, *The Spirit of Democratic Capitalism* (London, IEA Health and Welfare Unit, 1991).

20. ibid. p. 98.

21. ibid. p. 107.

22. ibid. p. 348.

23. Ronald H. Preston, *Religion and the Ambiguities of Capitalism* (London, SCM, 1991), p. 74.

24. Michael Novak, 'Eight arguments about the morality of the marketplace' in Jon Davies (ed.), *God and the Marketplace: essays on the morality of wealth creation* (London, IEA Health and Welfare Unit, 1993), pp. 24 ff.

25. Richard Roberts, 'The spirit of democratic capitalism: a critique of Michael Novak', in *God and the Marketplace*, p. 78.
26. Novak, 'Eight arguments', pp. 19 ff.
27. Richard Harries, *Is there a Gospel for the Rich?* (London, Mowbray, 1992), pp. 3 ff.
28. Peter Sedgwick, *The Enterprise Culture* (London, SPCK, 1992), p. 54.
29. ibid. p. 168.
30. John Atherton, *Christianity and the Market: Christian social thought for our time* (London, SPCK, 1992); see especially pp. 193 ff.
31. Preston, *Religion and the Ambiguities of Capitalism*, p. 145.
32. Stephen Green, *Serving God? Serving Mammon? Christians and the financial markets* (London, Marshall Pickering, 1996), p. 41, here quoting the Archbishop of Canterbury, Dr George Carey, in an address given to the Manchester Business School in 1994.
33. Dodd, *Sociology of Money*, see especially Chapter 2, 'Money and the State'.
34. ibid. p. 102.
35. J. K. Galbraith, *The Galbraith Reader* (Harmondsworth, Penguin, 1977), p. 482.
36. Will Hutton, *The State We're In* (London, Vintage, 1995), p. 68.
37. J. K. Galbraith, *The Culture of Contentment* (London, Sinclair-Stevenson, 1992), p. 43.
38. Galbraith caricatures this theory as the idea that if you feed the horse enough oats some will pass through to the road for the sparrows. See *The Culture of Contentment*, p. 108.
39. Hutton, *The State We're In*; see especially p. 243.
40. John C. Turmel has written about this in two generally available e-mail messages, 'Everything about banking and debt', an essay in plumbing and algebra applied to the banking system, and 'All about banking', a 670-verse ballad exposing the same deception at the heart of banking. He makes use of the concept of the 'piggy bank' too, but is rather less patronising about it. The material can be obtained from him at <bc726@ca.carleton.freenet>. See also Geoffrey Gardiner, *Towards True Monetarism* (London, Dulwich Press, 1993).
41. See Friedrich von Hayek, *The Denationalisation of Money* (London, IEA, 1976), discussed in Dodd, *Sociology of Money*, pp. 36 ff. On the limits to national freedom, see also David Lipsey, 'Taxing and spending' in Giles Radice (ed.), *What Needs to Change* (London, Harper Collins, 1996), pp. 124–39.
42. *Patriotic Money*, a series of four programmes, one each on sterling, the Deutschmark, the French franc and the dollar (broadcast by the BBC, August–September 1996).
43. Timothy J. Gorringe, *Capital and the Kingdom: theological ethics and economic order* (London, SPCK, 1994).

44. Duchrow, *Alternatives to Global Capitalism*.
45. ibid. p. 311.
46. ibid. p. 317.
47. Gorringe, *Capital and the Kingdom*, p. 167.
48. See for instance D. A. Hunter Johnston, *Stewardship and the Gospel* (1st edn May 1995, 2nd edn December 1995, privately distributed). I shall refer in the following chapter to this author's comments on usury.

Chapter 7: Forgotten wisdom

1. John Ruskin, extract from letter 68 in *Readings in Fors Clavigera* (Orpington, George Allen, 1899), p. 107. I am grateful for this and other relevant extracts from Ruskin's letters which have been republished by the Christian Council for Monetary Justice, 20 Nan Nook Road, Manchester M23 9BZ.
2. Dorothy Day, letter of July 1960, reprinted in *The Witness* 79.3 (March 1996), p. 6.
3. ibid.
4. Stephen Green, *Serving God? Serving Mammon? Christians and the financial markets* (London, Marshall Pickering, 1996), p. 39.
5. Timothy J. Gorringe, *Capital and the Kingdom: theological ethics and economic order* (London, SPCK, 1994), p. 167.
6. Justo L. González, *Faith and Wealth: a history of early Christian ideas on the origin, significance and use of money* (San Francisco, Harper & Row, 1990), p. 226.
7. Plutarch, *Lives and Writings: Plutarch's essays and miscellanea*, vol. 5 (London, Simpkin, Marshall, Hamilton, Kent, 1902), pp. 412–24.
8. Plutarch, *De vitando aere alien.* 4, quoted in González, *Faith and Wealth*, p. 13.
9. Aristotle, *Politics* 1258 a–b, quoted in González, *Faith and Wealth*, p. 10.
10. Cicero, *De Officiis*, 1.42; see González, *Faith and Wealth*, p. 16. On interest, see *Ad Atticum* V 21; VI 1; cf. R. M. Grant, *Early Christianity and Society: seven studies* (San Francisco, Harper & Row, 1977), p. 83.
11. Ronald Preston, *Religion and the Ambiguities of Capitalism* (London, SCM, 1991), p. 36.
12. See for instance the article on 'Usury' in F. L. Cross (ed.), *Oxford Dictionary of the Christian Church* (Oxford, Oxford University Press, 1958), p. 1401. For an evaluation of Luther and Calvin's positions, see G. K. Blount, *A Theology of Social Justice and Forgiveness in an Economic Context (Debt)* (Edinburgh University, unpublished PhD thesis, 1995), pp. 118 ff.
13. See above, Chapter 3, pp. 46–8.

14. The classic studies are by Max Weber, *The Protestant Ethic*, trans. Parsons (London, Allen & Unwin, 1930), and R. H. Tawney, *Religion and the Rise of Capitalism* (Harmondsworth, Penguin, 1938). See Gorringe, *Capital and the Kingdom*, p. 31.

15. D. A. Hunter-Johnston, *Stewardship and the Gospel* (1st edn May 1995, 2nd edn December 1995, privately distributed), pp. 79 ff. The author is able to be completely direct on the point: the 'enlightened and compassionate legislation' in the Old Testament 'has no bearing on straight business lending as we understand it today.'

16. Blount, *Social Justice and Forgiveness*, p. 102.

17. ibid. p. 99.

18. ibid. p. 103.

19. ibid. p. 105.

20. Bruce J. Malina, *The New Testament World: insights from cultural anthropology* (Atlanta, John Knox Press, 1981), p. 90.

21. Gerd Theissen, *The Shadow of the Galilean*, trans. John Bowden (London, SCM, 1987), p. 68.

22. ibid. fnn. 2 and 3, p. 204.

23. Richard A. Horsley, *Sociology and the Jesus Movement* (New York, Crossroad, 1989), p. 89.

24. ibid.

25. Douglas E. Oakman, *Jesus and the Economic Questions of his Day: studies in the Bible and early Christianity*, vol. 8 (Lewiston, Edwin Mellor, 1986), p. 74.

26. John Howard Yoder, *The Politics of Jesus* (Grand Rapids, Eerdmans, 1972), pp. 68 ff.

27. C. F. Evans, *The Lord's Prayer* (London, SPCK, 1963), pp. 57–63.

28. Oakman, *Jesus and the Economic Questions of his Day*, p. 155.

29. ibid.

30. John Kloppenburg, 'Alms, debt and divorce: Jesus' ethics in their Mediterranean context', *Toronto Journal of Theology* 6, p. 192 (article pp. 182–200), quoted in John Dominic Crossan, *The Historical Jesus: the life of a Mediterranean Jewish peasant* (Edinburgh, T. & T. Clark, 1991), p. 294.

31. Frances Young and David F. Ford, *Meaning and Truth in 2 Corinthians* (London, SPCK, 1987). See especially Chapter 6, 'The economy of God: exploring a metaphor'.

32. Graham Shaw, *The Cost of Authority: manipulation and freedom in the New Testament* (London, SCM, 1983), pp. 115–19.

33. C. K. Barrett, *Freedom and Obligation: a study of the Epistle to the Galatians* (London, SPCK, 1985), p. 70.

34. John Nicholson, *Words to a Liberating God* (printed privately, 1994); from 'Easter'.

Chapter 8: The economy of freedom

1. Carole B. Burgoyne and Stephen E. G. Lea, 'The psychology of Christmas' (*The Psychologist*, December 1995), p. 550.
2. Marcel Mauss, *The Gift* (Glencoe, Free Press, 1954).
3. David Cheal, *The Gift Economy* (London, Routledge, 1988), p. 183.
4. C. F. Evans, *The Lord's Prayer* (London, SPCK, 1963), p. 60.
5. John Milbank, 'Can a gift be given? Prolegomena to a future Trinitarian metaphysic', *Modern Theology* vol. 11.1 (January 1995), pp. 119–61.
6. For example, Jacques Derrida, *Given Time 1: Counterfeit Money* (Chicago, Chicago University Press, 1991); Jean-Luc Marion, *God Without Being* (Chicago, Chicago University Press, 1991).
7. Milbank, 'Can a gift be given?', p. 125.
8. ibid. p. 149.
9. Evans, *The Lord's Prayer*, p. 60.
10. Doctrine Commission of the Church of England, *The Mystery of Salvation* (London, Church House, 1995), p. 109.
11. From Abelard's Commentary on Romans; see E. R. Fairweather (ed.), *A Scholastic Miscellany* (London, SCM, 1956), pp. 276 ff. This text is quoted in Timothy Gorringe, *God's Just Vengeance: crime, violence and the rhetoric of salvation* (Cambridge, Cambridge University Press, 1996), p. 109.
12. Angela West, *Deadly Innocence: feminism and the mythology of sin* (London, Mowbray, 1995), p. 175.
13. ibid. p. 184.
14. ibid. p. 185.
15. Gorringe, *God's Just Vengeance*. For a similar concern for the development of 'recreative' rather than 'retributive' strategies in relation to the atonement, see Vernon White, *Atonement and Incarnation: an essay in universalism and particularity* (Cambridge, Cambridge University Press, 1991), especially Chapter 7, pp. 87–106.
16. I am grateful to Graham Blount for providing me with extracts from Mr Ewing's remarkable sermon 'On the duty of abstaining from debt'.
17. Boyd Hilton, *The Age of Atonement: the influence of evangelicalism on social and economic thought, 1785–1865* (Oxford, Clarendon, 1988), especially Chapters 4 and 5, pp. 115–202.
18. Gustav Aulén, *Christus Victor* (London, Macmillan, 1969).
19. J. Denny Weaver, 'Atonement for the nonConstantinian church', *Modern Theology* vol. 6.4 (July 1990), p. 316.
20. René Girard, *Things Hidden since the Foundation of the World* (Stamford, Stamford University Press, 1987), p. 209.
21. Dan Hardy, 'A magnificent complexity' in David F. Ford and Dennis L. Stamps (eds.), *Essentials of Christian Community: essays for Daniel W. Hardy* (Edinburgh, T. & T. Clark, 1996), pp. 325 ff.

22. Richard K. Fenn, *The Secularization of Sin: an investigation of the Daedalus complex* (Louisville, Westminster/John Knox Press, 1991), pp. 98 ff.
23. Robert Farrar Capon, *The Mystery of Christ . . . & why we don't get it* (Grand Rapids, Eerdmans, 1993), p. 27.
24. On this aspect see my *BeLonging: challenge to a tribal church* (London, SPCK, 1991).

Bibliography

Archbishop's Commission on Urban Priority Areas, *Faith in the City* (London, Church Information Office, 1985).

Arns, Carlo Evaristo, Archbishop of São Paulo, interview in *La Liberté*, 9 October 1985, quoted in Susan George, *A Fate Worse than Debt* (q.v.) p. 138.

Association of British Credit Unions, *Starting a Credit Union* (London, ABCU, 1989).

Credit Unions and You (London, ABCU, c.1987).

Atherton, John, *Christianity and the Market: Christian social thought for our time* (London, SPCK, 1992).

Aulén, Gustav, *Christus Victor* (London, Macmillan, 1969).

Barrett, C. K., *Freedom and Obligation: a study of the Epistle to the Galatians* (London, SPCK, 1985).

Berthoud, Richard, and Hinton, Teresa, *Credit Unions in the United Kingdom* (London, Policy Studies Research Unit Report 693, 1989).

Bethge, Eberhard, *Dietrich Bonhoeffer: a biography* (London, Collins, 1986).

Blount, Graham K., *A Theology of Social Justice and Forgiveness in an Economic Context (Debt)* (Edinburgh University, unpublished PhD thesis, 1995).

Bonhoeffer, Dietrich, 'Jesus Christ and the essence of Christianity', address of 11 December 1928, in G. B. Kelly and F. B. Nelson (eds.), *A Testament to Freedom* (San Francisco, Harper, 1990).

Sanctorum Communio: a dogmatic inquiry into the sociology of the Church (London, Collins, 1963).

Christology (London, Collins, 1966).

Letters and Papers from Prison, enlarged edition (London, SCM, 1971).

Bonhoeffer, Dietrich, and von Wedemeyer, Maria, *Love Letters from Cell 92* (London, Harper Collins, 1994).

Bovet, Theodor, *That They May Have Life: a handbook on pastoral care for Christian ministers and laymen* (London, DLT, 1964, trans. J. A. Baker from *Lebendige Seelsorge*, Verlag Paul Haupt, 1951).

Bowlby, R. O., *Third World Debt: what are the ethical issues?* (Essex University, unpublished lecture, January 1996).

Burgoyne, Carole B, and Lea, Stephen E. G., 'The psychology of Christmas', *The Psychologist* (December 1995).

Campbell, Beatrix, *Goliath: Britain's dangerous places* (London, Methuen, 1993).

Capon, Robert Farrar, *The Mystery of Christ . . . & Why We Don't Get It* (Grand Rapids, Eerdmans, 1993).

Centre for Theology and Public Issues, *Third World Debt – First World Responsibility* (Edinburgh, Centre for Theology and Public Issues, 1991).

Cheal, David, *The Gift Economy* (London, Routledge, 1988).

Christian Aid, *Banking on the Poor: the ethics of Third World debt* (London, 1991).

Clements, Keith, *A Patriotism for Today* (London, Collins, 1986).

Copley, David, and Spray, Paul, *Who God Bless, Let No Man Curse – Jamaica: health and debt* (London, Christian Aid, 1995).

Cross, F. L. (ed.), *Oxford Dictionary of the Christian Church* (Oxford, Oxford University Press, 1958).

Crossan, John Dominic, *The Historical Jesus: the life of a Mediterranean Jewish peasant* (Edinburgh, T. & T. Clark, 1991).

Crowther Report, *Consumer Credit* (London, HMSO, 1971).

Cullmann, O., *Christ and Time* (London, SCM, 1962).

Davies, Emma, and Lea, Stephen E. G., 'Student attitudes to student debt', *Journal of Economic Psychology* 16 (1995).

Davies, John D., *World on Loan* (London, Bible Society, 1993).

Davies, Jon (ed.), *God and the Marketplace: essays on the morality of wealth creation* (London, IEA Health and Welfare Unit, 1993).

Davis, Richard, and Dhooge, Yvonne, *Living with Mortgage Arrears* (London, HMSO, 1993).

Day, Dorothy, letter from *The Catholic Worker*, reprinted in *The Witness* 79.3 (March 1996).

de Gruchy, John W., 'Bonhoeffer in South Africa', explanatory essay in Bethge, Eberhard, *Bonhoeffer: exile and martyr* (London, Collins, 1975).

Bonhoeffer and South Africa: theology in dialogue (Grand Rapids, Eerdmans, 1984).

Dietrich Bonhoeffer: witness to Jesus Christ (London, Collins, 1988).

Christianity and Democracy (Cambridge, Cambridge University Press, 1995).

de Gruchy, John W. (ed.), *Bonhoeffer for a New Day: theology in a time of transition* (Grand Rapids, Eerdmans, 1997).

Dent, M. J., *Jubilee 2000 and Lessons of the World Debt Tables (1992–93 and 1993–94)* (published by the author, Dept of Politics, Keele University, 1994).

'The debt tables of the World Bank', *Journal of Modern African Studies* 32.4 (1994).

'Theological help in an urgent economic crisis', *Crucible* (January to March 1994).

Derrida, Jacques, *Given Time 1: Counterfeit Money* (Chicago, Chicago University Press, 1991).

Doctrine Commission of the Church of England, *The Mystery of Salvation* (London, Church House Publishing, 1995).

Dodd, Nigel, *The Sociology of Money: economics, reason and contemporary Society* (New York, Continuum, 1994).

Doling, J., Ford, J. and Stafford, B., *Property Owing Democracy* (Aldershot, Gower, 1988).

Doling, J., and Stafford, B., *Home Ownership: the diversity of experience* (Aldershot, Gower, 1989).

Duchrow, Ulrich, *Alternatives to Global Capitalism: drawn from biblical history, designed for political action* (Utrecht, International Books, 1995).

Duncan, Alan, and Hobson, Dominic, *Saturn's Children: how the State devours liberty, prosperity and virtue* (London, Sinclair Stevenson, 1995).

Ellul, Jacques, *The Meaning of the City* (Grand Rapids, Eerdmans, 1970).

Equiano, Olaudah, '*Autobiography*' in Paul Edwards and David Dabydeen (eds.), *Black Writers in Britain 1769–1890: an anthology* (Edinburgh, Edinburgh University Press, 1991, reprinted 1995).

Etchegaray, Roger, *Millennium Jubilee: church event – challenge to society*, the tenth Pope Paul VI Memorial Lecture (London, CAFOD, 1996).

Evans, C. F., *The Lord's Prayer* (London, SPCK, 1963).

Fenn, Richard K., *The Secularization of Sin: an investigation of the Daedalus complex* (Louisville, Westminster/John Knox Press, 1991).

Finnis, N., 'Mortgage arrears: tomorrow's problems', *Roof* (January 1978).

Ford, David F., 'Faith in the cities: Corinth and the modern city' in D. W. Hardy and C. E. Gunton, *On Being the Church* (q.v.).

Ford, David F., and Stamps, Dennis L., *Essentials of Christian Community* (Edinburgh, T. & T. Clark, 1996).

Galbraith, J. K., *The Galbraith Reader* (Harmondsworth, Penguin, 1977).

The Culture of Contentment (London, Sinclair Stevenson, 1992).

Gardiner, Geoffrey, *Towards True Monetarism* (London, Dulwich Press, 1993).

George, Susan, *The Debt Boomerang: how Third World debt harms us all* (London, Pluto, 1992).

A Fate Worse than Debt: a radical analysis of the Third World debt crisis (Harmondsworth, Penguin, 1994).

George, Susan, and Sabelli, Fabrizio, *Faith and Credit: the World Bank's secular empire* (Harmondsworth, Penguin, 1994).

Girard, René, *Things Hidden Since the Foundation of the World* (Stamford, Stamford University Press, 1987).

González, Justo L., *Faith and Wealth: a history of early Christian ideas on the origin, significance and use of money* (San Francisco, Harper & Row, 1977).

Gorringe, Timothy J., *Capital and the Kingdom: theological ethics and economic order* (London, SPCK, 1994).

God's Just Vengeance: crime, violence and the rhetoric of salvation (Cambridge, Cambridge University Press, 1996).

Grant, R. M., *Early Christianity and Society: seven studies* (San Francisco, Harper & Row, 1977).

Green, Stephen, *Serving God? Serving Mammon? Christians and the financial markets* (London, Marshall Pickering, 1996).

Gwynne, S. C., 'Adventures in the loan trade', *Harper's Magazine* (September 1988).

Hardy, Daniel W., 'Sociality created and redeemed' in D. W. Hardy and C. E. Gunton, *On Being the Church* (q.v.).

'A magnificent complexity' in David F. Ford and Dennis L. Stamps, *Essentials of Christian Community* (q.v.).

Hardy, D. W., and Gunton, C. E., *On Being the Church: essays on Christian community* (Edinburgh, T & T Clark, 1989).

Harries, Richard, *Is there a Gospel for the Rich?* (London, Mowbray, 1992).

Hayek, F., *The Denationalisation of Money* (London, IEA, 1976).

Hilton, Boyd, *The Age of Atonement: the influence of evangelicalism on social and economic thought, 1785–1865* (Oxford, Clarendon Press, 1988).

Hirst, Paul, and Thompson, Grahame, *Globalization in Question: the international economy and the possibilities of governance* (Cambridge, Polity Press, 1996).

Horsley, Richard A., *Sociology and the Jesus Movement* (New York, Crossroad, 1989).

Hull, John M., 'Christian education in a capitalist society: money and God' in David F. Ford and Dennis L. Stamps, *Essentials of Christian Community* (q.v.).

Hunter-Johnston, D. A., *Stewardship and the Gospel* (1st edn May 1995, 2nd edn December 1995, privately distributed).

Hutton, Will, *The State We're In* (London, Vintage Books, 1995).

Jenkins, David E., 'Concerning theism' in John A. T. Robinson and David L. Edwards (eds.), *The Honest to God Debate* (London, SCM Press, 1963)

Joseph, M. P., 'A Third World viewpoint' in Centre for Theology and Public Issues, *Third World Debt – First World Responsibility* (q.v.).

Jubilee Trust, *Escaping the Debt Trap: the problem of consumer credit and debt in Britain today* (Cambridge, Jubilee Trust, 1990).

Kloppenburg, John, 'Alms, debt and divorce: Jesus' ethics in the Mediterranean context', *Toronto Journal of Theology* 6, quoted in John Dominic Crossan, *The Historical Jesus* (q.v.).

Lea, Stephen E. G., Webley, Paul, and Walker, Catherine M., 'Psychological factors in consumer debt: money management, economic socialization and credit use', *Journal of Economic Psychology* 16 (1995).

Lipsey, David, 'Taxing and spending', in Giles Radice (ed.), *What Needs to Change* (London, Harper Collins, 1996).

MacDonald, Alison, 'Down and out in Hawthorn Avenue', *Woman* (9 March 1985), quoted in Doling *et al.*, *Property Owing Democracy* (q.v.).

Malina, Bruce J., *The New Testament World: insight from cultural anthropology* (Atlanta, John Knox Press, 1981).

Mannion, Russell, *Dealing with Debt: an evaluation of money advice services* (London, HMSO, 1992).

Marion, Jean-Luc, *God Without Being* (Chicago, Chicago University Press, 1991).

Mauss, Marcel, *The Gift* (Glencoe, Free Press, 1954).

Milbank, John, 'Can a gift be given? Prolegomena to a future Trinitarian metaphysic', *Modern Theology* 11.1 (January 1995).

Morton, Andrew R. (ed.), *Domestic Debt: disease of consumer society* (Edinburgh, Centre for Theology and Public Issues, 1996).

National Association of Citizens' Advice Bureaux, *The Cost of Living: CAB evidence on debt and poverty* (1992).

National Consumer Council, *Consumers and Credit* (London, HMSO, 1980).

Credit and Debt: the consumer interest (London, HMSO, 1990).

Nicholson, John, *Words to a Liberating God* (privately distributed).

Nietzsche, Friedrich, *A Genealogy of Morals* (London, T. Fisher Unwin, 1899).

Novak, Michael, *The Spirit of Democratic Capitalism* (London, IEA Health and Welfare Unit, 1991).

'Eight arguments about the morality of the marketplace' in Jon Davies (ed.), *God and the Marketplace: essays on the morality of wealth creation* (q.v.).

Nygren, Anders, *Agape and Eros* (London, SPCK, 1982).

Oakman, Douglas E., *Jesus and the Economic Questions of his Day: studies in the Bible and early Christianity*, vol. 8 (Lewiston, Edwin Mellor Press, 1986).

Open University, *An Introduction to Credit Unions*, a resource pack (Milton Keynes, Open University, 1991).

Patriotic Money, four programmes on money (broadcast by the BBC, August–September 1996).

Pettifor, Ann, *Debt: the most potent form of slavery* (London, Debt Crisis Network, 1996).

'Jubilee and the remission of debts: the Churches and a new fight against slavery', submission to the 1996 Bossey Conference on Jubilee (unpublished).

Phipps, Simon, ordination sermon (unpublished, June 1990).

Preston, Ronald, *Religion and the Ambiguities of Capitalism* (London, SCM, 1991).

Provident Financial, Annual report, *Independent* (31 August 1995).

Ramsey, A. M., Sermon to the Modern Churchmen's Conference, 24 July 1967, in *Christ for us Today: papers from the Fiftieth Annual Conference of Modern Churchmen* (London, SCM, 1968).

Roberts, Richard, 'The spirit of democractic capitalism: a critique of Michael Novak' in Jon Davies (ed.), *God and the Marketplace: essays on the morality of wealth creation* (q.v.).

Ruskin, John, *Readings in Fors Clavigera* (Orpington, George Allen, 1899).

Schluter, Michael, and Lee, David, *Credit and Debt: sorting it out* (London, Marshall Pickering, 1989).

Sedgwick, Peter, *The Enterprise Culture* (London, SPCK, 1992).

Selby, Peter, 'Saved through hope', *Christian Action Journal* (Summer 1986).

Belonging: Challenge to a Tribal Church (London, SPCK, 1991).

'What Simeon said . . . and Anna was waiting for' in Eric James, Chris Rowland, and Peter Selby (eds.), in 'The Gospel, the Poor and the Churches: Reflections for a Jubilee' (*Christian Action Journal*, Autumn 1995).

Shaw, Graham, *The Cost of Authority: manipulation and freedom in the New Testament* (London, SCM, 1983).

Simmel, Georg, *The Philosophy of Money* (London, Routledge & Kegan Paul, 1978), trans. Tom Bottomore and David Frisby from *Philosophie des Geldes* (Berlin, 1907).

Smith, Dan, 'The fifth boomerang: immigration', in Susan George, *The Debt Boomerang* (q.v.).

Spray, Paul, 'The abolition of the international debt trade' in Centre for Theology and Public Issues, *Third World Debt – First World Responsibility* (q.v.).

Student Money Project, *Report* (London, University of Exeter and National Westminster Bank, 1994).

Taylor, Michael, *Not Angels but Agencies: the ecumenical response to poverty – a primer* (London, SCM, 1995).

Theissen, Gerd, *The Shadow of the Galilean*, trans. John Bowden (London, SCM, 1987).

Thomas, Lyn C., 'A management science perspective' in Andrew R. Morton (ed.), *Domestic Debt: disease of consumer society* (Edinburgh, Centre for Theology and Public Issues, 1996).

Turmel, John C., 'Everything about banking and debt' and 'All about banking', articles obtainable by electronic mail from the author at <bc726@ca.carleton.freenet>.

UNICEF, *The State of the World's Children* (1989).

Weaver, J. Denny, 'Atonement for the nonConstantinian Church', *Modern Theology* 6.4 (July 1990).

West, Angela, *Deadly Innocence: feminism and the mythology of sin* (London, Mowbray, 1995).

White, Vernon, *Atonement and Incarnation: an essay in universalism and particularity* (Cambridge, Cambridge University Press, 1991).

Williams, Brian, *Cleaning up the Debt Environment: policies for the prevention of debt among low income families* (Cambridge, Jubilee Centre Publications, 1990).

Willmer, Haddon, 'Bonhoeffer's sanctity as a problem for Bonhoeffer studies' in *Celebrating Critical Awareness: Bonhoeffer and Bradford 60 years on* (London, International Bonhoeffer Society, 1993).

Wolfe, Michael, *Handbook of Debt Advice* (London, Child Poverty Action Group, 1996).

Yoder, John Howard, *The Politics of Jesus* (Grand Rapids, Eerdmans, 1972).

Young, Frances, and Ford, David F., *Meaning and Truth in 2 Corinthians* (London, SPCK, 1987).

Index